Time
Management
Ninja

Time Management Ninja

21 Tips for More Time and Less Stress in Your Life

Craig Jarrow

CORAL GABLES, FL

Published by Mango Publishing, a division of Mango Publishing Group, Inc.

Cover Design: Morgane Leoni
Interior Design: Jermaine Lau

For permission requests, please contact the publisher at:

Mango Publishing Group
2850 S Douglas Road, 4th Floor
Coral Gables, FL 33134 USA
info@mango.bz

For special orders, quantity sales, course adoptions and corporate sales, please email the publisher at sales@mango.bz. For trade and wholesale sales, please contact Ingram Publisher Services at: customer.service@ingramcontent.com or +1.800.509.4887.

Time Management Ninja: 21 Tips for More Time and Less Stress in Your Life

Library of Congress Cataloging-in-Publication number: 2019944128
ISBN: (p) 978-1-63353-891-7 (e) 978-1-63353-892-4
BISAC: SEL035000—SELF-HELP / Self-Management / Time Management

Printed in the United States of America

TABLE OF CONTENTS

FOREWORD

Throughout my many years in the time management world, I have been fortunate to meet many productivity authors who have helped others reclaim their time and lives. However, few have been as passionate about living a simple and purposeful life as Craig.

This book is about taking control of your life by better managing the time you have. It is about using the right tools to get the job done while reducing effort and stress. It is about using the right tools to find peace in life.

Time Management Ninja draws from Craig's platform of the same name, where for over ten years he has written about time management. His international readership appreciates his straightforward strategies and simple, laser focused, ninja-like solutions.

This book teaches twenty-one tips which are designed to help you in your daily activities and planning. In many ways, this is the "missing" time management class that people wish they were taught in school. It also contains lessons to help guide you to achieve your goals and in living a purposeful life.

Craig and I connected online many years ago, after I had seen his time management blog. Once we started corresponding, I learned that I had been a mentor to his efforts. He had been an avid follower of my time management teachings, and a big user of Franklin DayPlanners back in the day.

I am honored to have been the source of much of his inspiration and have watched as Craig has grown his online brand and become a well-known expert in the productivity field.

If you apply what you learn in *Time Management Ninja*, I promise you that Craig's twenty-one tips will help you be better at managing your time and life. Whether that is to accomplish your life's dreams or simply be more organized in your daily planning, this guide will allow you to get more done with less effort.

Time is the only resource we don't get more. I hope you follow Craig's advice and spend yours wisely!

HYRUM SMITH

Author of *The 10 Natural Laws of Successful Time and Life Management* and *Purposeful Retirement*

INTRODUCTION

"I don't have enough time."

"I am so tired from trying to catch up, I'll never get ahead."

"I don't get to the important things in my life because I am too busy."

Sound familiar? No, it's not telepathy. As a time management ninja, I've heard this all before. But your fears are going to be conquered! Your training begins now.

These days, our lives appear to be endless marathons of busyness. It feels like there is never enough time to get to what's important, which means we have even *less* time to do what we actually enjoy!

On top of that, you probably spend more time scrolling through dozens of perfect #beachday posts or "chilling with your phone" than getting work done with it. And even when you *do* finally try to get work done, it interrupts you many times an hour. (Or minute!) It's sneaky[1] when it does it, too, so when you innocently open up your screen time report, you're taken aback. Yes, you actually *did* spend five hours on Facebook. *What?!*

But you know this already. More than likely, you have already *tried* to better manage your time. You've scoured the

---

1   It's stealthy, sure, but soon you'll be the ninja in the relationship. Read on.

app store, bookstore, and online for any semblance of hope, but instead found that most time management systems are way too complicated or simply don't fit in with your routine and workload. So, you stopped using them almost as quickly as you picked them up. Delete, and then move on. It's a vicious cycle. Meanwhile, your time is ticking away.

If you are tired of always rushing, letting technology dominate your time, and procrastinating when you should be working...*then this book is for you*!

The Time Crisis

You are not alone in feeling that you don't have enough time in your day.

Everyone is too busy. In fact, our *society* is busier than ever.

A recent study found that the average adult has just over *four hours* per week of free time. That is not much time at all to spend on personal tasks and goals. Yet, your whole life is made up of personal tasks and goals! *Those* are your dreams. How much time are you spending on them, on average? Four. Hours.

It's a dreary reality. No, we can't deny it—there is a growing time crisis. Quite frankly, the lack of time in people's personal lives has become an epidemic. People have less time to themselves. That means less time to do what's important, whether that is to work on life goals or spend precious time with family and loved ones.

Our modern daily lives consist of constant interruptions, notifications, and calls for our attention. We spend more of our days "plugged in" to streams of requests, information, and news than we do on the tasks that make us feel alive.

If you are like most, you spend your entire day reacting to the stimuli around you. And when you *do* finally reach the end of your day, it often seems like you have accomplished nothing of consequence. No kidding. You have spent the whole day *reacting* instead of *acting*.

It seems there is never any time to just *think*. Or to actually do what is important to you. Ultimately, it feels as though the world is in an ongoing battle for our attention. Our devices distract us dozens of times per hour, telling us about things that "just can't wait." Most people can't go more than a minute or two without being interrupted.

If you doubt this, I dare you to try the following experiment. What is the experiment, you ask? Paying attention. Right, seems easy enough. Well, what if I told you that *most people will not make it to the end before their attention wanders or they receive an interruption?* Not fazed? Feeling testy? Try it. I *dare* you.

Take this seriously and concentrate.

Slowly and deliberately count to ten. Take a breath between each number. *And do nothing else*. You only have to reach ten.

How did it go? Most importantly, how far did you get before you got distracted? Before you remembered a task you urgently have to do? Someone you have to call? Felt the itch to be doing *something*?

Chances are, you didn't make it.

Perhaps, your mind wandered to that task (*really should get my dog washed before algae grows*). Or your phone buzzed with a news notification (*another escaped sea lion?*). Or your email dinged to let you know of a new message (*50% off all SALE items! Buy now! Please!*).

Doesn't matter what specifically distracted you...the fact that you *were* is the point. We live in a world of endless diversions that keep us from being productive.

It is truly a scary way to live. Yet...

Technology Was Supposed to Make Things Easier!

The searing irony of the time crisis is that we were supposed to have *more time* by now. The future was supposed to bring technology that would make our lives carefree and effortless. Technology was supposed to make us *more* productive. It was supposed to do the work *for* us. Gadgets, apps, robots, artificial intelligence...it was all intended to make our lives easier!

Instead, the very technology that was supposed to save us has taken over our lives. It acts as a leash on our work, pulling us back and stopping us in our tracks no matter where we are.

If you think we aren't living in *The Matrix*, here's the red pill—many people spend *over ten hours per day using their technology*. Picking up the phone is easy. Scrolling is second nature. Now try putting the technology *down.* What happens when you do? The glittery screen beeps, chimes, or vibrates *begging* you to come back. These artificial beings are controlling us, distracting us with this fabricated reality while they suck our life force. Too far?

Most can't go more than a minute or two without a distraction. I bet that while you have been reading this introduction your phone has made a noise interrupting your attention.

Now, technology isn't *all* bad. As any superhero movie will tell you—any powerful thing can be used for good or ridden to ruin.

Yes, we have harnessed the virtues of technology for quite a lot of good. Needless to say, it's thanks to automation and electronics that we can do things that before were unthinkable. We can work from almost anywhere. We can communicate in ways never before imagined. *And* we have access to the entire world's information in the palm of our hand. The devastating loss of knowledge, like in the burning of the library in Alexandria, is a concern of the past.

Of course, this open access is good. In moderation. Between social networks, endless news, and push notifications...our devices often take up more time than they give back.

I sometimes joke that many people have "affairs" with their phones.

Think about it. They spend more time with their phones than with their loved ones. They *sleep with* their phones. It is often the last thing they look at before they go to bed and the first thing they look at when they wake up. It's time to tell your partner you "met someone."

We are already living in *The Matrix*. The automatons provide us with a superficial, endless source of interruptions, notifications, and time-consuming information. Yes, they are slowly fabricating a new reality, and extracting our life-force while they're at it. Only difference is, we're sentient and we're letting them.

Time Management Shouldn't Be Difficult

Like I mentioned in the beginning, if you're picking up this book it's likely you have already tried to fight back against the endless bouts of procrastination and distractions. Yes, you have already tried to manage your time—or tried to use an app or system to do it for you.

However, the more you *try*, the more time you *spend* on gadgets and systems that end up taking more time than they give back. It's a toxic relationship.

Likely, you've used apps that have such a steep learning curve or so many required actions that you became frustrated. Or techniques that are so complex that they require a flowchart. *A flowchart!*

You use them for a few days and then realize that they aren't sustainable or realistic. They quickly end up in a drawer. Just like that, you're back where you started. The only progress made? Finding out that none of them work for you. Why is managing your time so difficult?

But that's a loaded question. The answer is...*it shouldn't be*.

Time management should be effortless. Smooth. Ninja-like. It isn't something that you "turn on" when you are behind on your work. It should be part of your life and as easy as your other daily habits, like brushing your teeth. *That* easy.

Your time-saving system should also be as simple as common sense. A streamlined approach will beat a complicated system every time. Get ready to master some defyingly simple time ninja moves.

And no, you *won't* need a flowchart.

Reclaiming Your Time

It's *your* time.

You don't have to give it up and away. You don't have to let others steal it. You're in control.

It is time to do something about the time crisis and the technology takeover. It is time to better manage your life. Ninja kick your way through this.

This book will give you twenty-one simple tips to give you back time back in your life. Inevitably, you will experience less stress as you begin to unplug from the endless stream of distractions.

So, if you are ready to reclaim your time and life, then let's get started!

TIME MANAGEMENT

SHOULD MAKE TIME, NOT

TAKE TIME

---

*Your time management moves should free up more
time than it requires in your day.*

"I don't have time to plan for my day."

You say this while drowning in work, obligations, and appointments. How could you possibly have extra time to *manage* your time when you're so busy doing everything else?

The truth is that you, quite frankly, don't have time *not* to manage your time. What, you don't have time to make sure you have more time? There is so much at stake.

The purpose of stealthy time-saving is to give you time back. It's about using your hours effectively and getting your most important work done first.

The "I don't have enough time!" statement is an excuse for not taking charge of your day. It's a cheap line for not living a purposeful life. When you practice proper productivity habits, you aren't expending more precious minutes and hours—you are seizing them back.

Get More Time for Your Life

You have the same amount of time every day. In fact, we all do.

24 hours. 1,440 minutes. 86,400 seconds.

Wouldn't it be great if you had an extra hour in your day? How about two? Or even three? Suddenly, the world opens up. It's kind of like fantasizing about winning the lottery.

Except...managing your time properly is *far* more likely to happen. You can win the time lottery! You can get precious moments back. The time you are losing each day.

Time that you are wasting on procrastination or, frankly, unnecessary activities.

Now here's the first lottery number. The first ninja move, my grasshopper. *Any attempt to manage your time must give you back more time than it takes.*

Yes, you must invest time in planning your activities, but the return that investment brings should be more than it requires upfront.

This means your system needs to be *simple*.

Make it Easy and Breezy

In addition to the "not enough time" excuse, the runner-up is "effective planning is too difficult."

Okay, so maybe some of you believe this whole time-saving thing is just too hard. Well, it doesn't help when those who *do* try to manage their time are left at the "try" phase. They give up because their systems are *just too complicated*. Those systems are the ones that scare potential time-savers away. How could you realistically be expected to micro-manage your day to the second? Or *worse*, be expected to plan *every detail* of the next five years? Ahhh!

Time management shouldn't require a flowchart. It doesn't need Zen philosophies. Or memorizing matrices of next actions (whatever that means).

Instead, effective planning should be simple. Only *that* way can it fit into your lifestyle and daily activities seamlessly. When done correctly, it becomes a sleek ninja routine that you can keep up effortlessly.

Always Be Time-Mindful

Another misconception about time management is that it is something you only "turn on" when you need it. Preferably, it is a set of habits that are part of your daily activities. You head out to jog, apply time management. You sneak a nap in, apply time management. Time management for you, and you, and you.

The truth is, you won't need to "turn it on" because soon you will learn how to always live a life that incorporates the most effective productivity principles. This knowledge and its application will allow you to manage your life more easily.

When you incorporate effective planning into your daily lifestyle, others will look to you as the model of how things should get done. And they will be in awe of how easily you seem to stay on top of your workload. How does that sound?

Simplicity Is Best

When approaching time management for the first time, many beginners are overwhelmed. I don't blame them. Google "time management apps" and you'll generate 1.86 billion results.

Another great irony—some of the most popular methodologies for a productive life are also the most cumbersome and complicated.

Your life already has too much going on, *why* would you want to add more difficulty?

As mentioned before, a good rule of thumb is, "If your time management requires a flow chart, it is too complicated."

Are you *really* going to refer to a chart every time you are trying to get organized? It definitely shouldn't take you thirty minutes to prioritize and sort your to-do list into a matrix either.

A good set of necessary weapons, used with discipline, will beat a complicated system any day of the week.

When it comes to time management, the simplest solution is the best.

Common sense and practical tools (the best weapons for the war against wasted time) will make you more successful than a system that takes weeks to learn and years to implement. Managing your time should be quick, effortless, and efficient.

So, as you start to create an effective plan for controlling your time, keep Tip 1 in mind. Keep. Things. Simple.

In the next chapter, we will examine the time management weapons that you will need to be as productive as possible. With the right training and mindset, you will become a stealthy time management ninja in no time.

Ninja Wisdom

✖ Time management should give back more time than it takes.

✖ Using time effectively should be an easy habit that is part of your daily routine.

✖ The simplest productivity solutions are the most effective.

Ninja Training

If you are telling yourself that you don't have time for time management, ask yourself the following questions:

✖ Are you genuinely practicing time management each and every day or are you only giving it lip service?

✖ When and where do you do your planning and preparation? (We will delve into these topics in future chapters.) Do you think your current planning routine is helping you? In what ways?

✖ Where and on what do you waste time each day?

✖ Where do you see opportunities to reclaim time in your day?

✖ What would you do with an extra two hours in your day? Be specific. Make a list of the activities, projects, or goals that you would spend this time on.

TIME MANAGEMENT ISN'T A LIGHT SWITCH

Do you turn on your time management when you are in a jam? Only to turn it back off once it is the weekend or when you are past the obstacle?

That method works just as well as cramming for a test. Sure, it *might* work in the short-term. But suddenly it's a few days after you data-dumped all of your last-minute knowledge on the test, and you're totally ignorant on the subject again. It's not sustainable. Not very useful if you want to consistently save more time.

Put quite simply, time management is *not* a quick one-time fix.

Far too many people try to use it that way. They think, "I'll save more time when I need to and then slack off later. *I deserve it!*" Then you wonder why you still feel totally unproductive.

Clearly, this technique does not work very well. Yet, in desperate attempts to get their lives back in order, people find themselves continually climbing back on the time management bandwagon.

In order to organize your time effectively, you need to make the active, daily effort to consistently use your time productively. In short, time management needs to be a habit.

Here are a few reasons why people try to turn their time management on and off:

✘ **It Is Too Complex**: Many people find that their system is just too complicated. How can a convoluted plan ever be sustainable? Suddenly, the more efficient option becomes forgoing the plan altogether.

✗ **It Is Not Life-Oriented**: If your system does not cover the needs of your day-to-day activities, you will quickly stop using it. Many people will try to use an incomplete system and subsequently give it up because it is "not working." No kidding! Your system is supposed to help you. Not be a decorative statement.

✗ **It Does Not Have Tools They Will Realistically Use**: Often people try to jump on the latest craze without considering if the device is one that they will *actually* use. Why buy the newest smartphone if you could do better with a paper-based solution? If you want a system that will work for you, then it is vital to pick tools that you are good with and enjoy using. Otherwise, they will end up as paperweights on a desk or in the "miscellaneous" drawer (we all know everything in that drawer is junk). How else could you efficiently destroy time-wasting?

✗ **It Is a Skill**: Time management is a skill that you must practice with tenacity. Like mastering any musical instrument or skateboard move, it takes rehearsal and experience. The more you do it, the swifter of a time-saver you will become.

✗ **The Myth of the Crisis**: There is no one-time crisis. Every day, you are *consistently* wasting time. Our war is constant. It's a state of being. Time-wasting doesn't occur in the just one moment of "disaster" when you space out for thirty minutes. People tend to think they only need time management in a jam. But the truth is...*you need it just as much when you are not in a crisis.* Planning your time is a proactive action that prevents the problems in the first place. Having the weapons handy helps you keep up the stealthy time-saving habit.

Time management is really life management. You can't turn it on and off and expect results (sounds like dieting, right?). Instead, keep your time management "on" at all times. Inevitably, you will find that the skills will naturally become a part of your healthy lifestyle.

HOW MUCH TIME CAN YOU RECLAIM?

People are often surprised by just how much time they can get back in their day. Think of getting back thirty minutes. Maybe one hour? Go higher. I would say that the average person can give back *two full hours* to their schedule.

That is significant. I am positive you can think of countless important things you could do with those two hours. Here's a list to get started:

✗ Workout

✗ Pursue a goal

✗ Meditate or journal

✗ Complete those procrastinated tasks on your list

✗ Catch up on cleaning or other chores

✗ Have fun! What have you been wanting to do but haven't had time for?

These are just a few examples that I am sure pop to mind. However, it's *much* bigger than that. It's not *just* about getting two hours back.

Instead, it's about getting two hours back *each and every day*.

Suddenly, you are talking about an extra fourteen (!) hours a week. Or sixty hours a month. Assuming you have an eight-hour workday, that is *seven and a half* workdays!

Or how about 730 hours per year! That is a mind-blowing 91 working days a year. What could you accomplish now? Suddenly the options become much more ambitious:

✘ Get a degree

✘ Write a book

✘ Learn a new language

✘ Start a business

When you consider how much time you can reclaim in your life, you will wonder what you have been doing until now!

TIP 2
_____

YOU NEED FOUR

PRODUCTIVITY WEAPONS

_____

To get more done with less effort, you need the
right productivity weapons.

_____

What tools or gadgets do you use to manage your time?

Do you use your phone as your primary device? Or do you carry a paper-based planner with you? Paper or technology solutions can be equally good. Whatever you choose, you must ensure that you have the right set of tools at your disposal.

You simply can't fight a war against wasted time without the right weapons. You can *try*, but you will spend an unnecessary amount of time and effort that won't help you produce your best results. That enemy—wasting time—is ruthless. Unforgiving. Combatting it takes skill and advanced weaponry. Weaponry that is sleek, effective, and defyingly simple.

You can *try* to be better with your time and work, but you just won't reach your full potential *unless you unsheathe the most brutal, yet simple, defense mechanisms.*

There are four essential weapons that you need in your stronghold. They aren't surprising, and you are likely familiar with each of them.

What *is* surprising, though, is that you are probably missing at least *one* of these. Know what that means? Missing even one of these means you are not going to be nearly as effective as you could be if you had all them. You have to go in full force.

Do you have each of the following?

Four Essential Weapons

You will need these with you *at all times*. Without all of them, you cannot manage your time effectively and constantly. You must be a constant threat to procrastination. Individually, each is a powerful instrument that will help you get your work done. Together, they are a complete set crafted with one purpose—get more done with less effort.

You already know the four essential time management weapons. After all, they are quite common. The tough question is, "Do you have each of these readily available at all times?"

Have these on your person at all times:

1. **To-do List:** A to-do list is crucial for tracking your tasks and obligations. Your to-do list should remember your tasks so that your mind is free to work on what is immediately in front of you.

2. **Calendar:** Your calendar should track your schedule and remind you when and where you need to be. While you are living in the now, your calendar can follow your appointments that are days, weeks, or even years in advance.

3. **Address Book:** Even in our technology-driven world, having people's contact information is imperative so that we may be able to connect with others. Your address book captures those contact details so you will have them at your fingertips in the future.

31

4. **Notebook**: A good notebook records your most important information. The idea here is that you have one notebook to record your notes so that you are not writing things down in random places or on Post-it Notes that can get easily misplaced.

None of these instruments is new or groundbreaking. You've had some version of each at some time. Maybe they are scattered between your home and office. Or perhaps, you have *multiple* of each, depending on your circumstances.

The important thing about Tip 2 is that you need each of these weapons, and you need to have them available to you at all times.

The Power of One

Sure, you need a to-do list, calendar, address book, and notebook, but is it possible to have *too* many? Absolutely. Having too many tools for the same purpose can be very confusing.

While most people are missing at least one of these, it is *just* as important that you do not have more than one. Multiple weapons of the same type add complexity, duplicity, and extra effort.

Have you ever missed an appointment because you had it on your *other* calendar? Or forgotten a task because you started a separate list that you left behind somewhere?

Surplus tools will actually slow you down and make you *less* productive.

You need only one of each type of productivity weapon.

I call this the "Power of One."

One to-do list. One calendar. One address book. And one notebook.

You should only have one of each type. Otherwise, you are merely creating extra burden and effort for yourself.

Choose Weapons You'll *Actually* Use

When someone is selecting their time management weapons, they inevitably ask the question, "Which tools are best?"

Don't get hung up on picking your tools. Go with the simplest time management weapons that you like.

Is a day-planner effective? Should I use a phone app?

The answer is...it depends.

It depends on your personal situation, your work environment, and more. But, most important, it depends on *you*. You may be more comfortable using a paper notebook and pen versus an app on your phone. Or maybe your workplace practically lives by email and an electronic means is just better suited to save time. The main thing is to choose tools that suit your desires, skills, and environment.

In other words, *always choose tools that you will actually use.*

You should pick your time management weapons based on what you *like*, not which is the most advanced. If you aren't comfortable or good at using them, you won't stick with them. More likely than not, they will end up "accidentally" in a trash can or left behind in the rental car (oops?).

Paper or Phone?

One of the big questions that comes up when first choosing time management weapons is, "Should I choose a paper-based or electronic solution?"

For a long time, paper-based solutions were the only option. But technology now offers many pretty powerful options.

So, which is better? A paper day-planner or a phone-based app?

As before...it depends. Don't get frustrated with this apparent non-answer.

In this day and age, it would *seem* like a phone app would be the best solution. For better or for worse, our devices are at the center of our lives. We carry them everywhere we go. How many times have you realized you left your phone at home and made a James Bond style U-turn? Yes, you can find most people within a few feet of their phones.

This makes a strong case for a device-based system. Your weapons have to be with you to be effective, and we all have our phones with us. So, this is a natural fit. Not to mention, the ability to sync across devices and locations makes your time management even *more* omnipresent. You can have your information synced to your home and work devices. This eliminates the redundancy that occurs when one has multiple productivity tools in different locations. It embodies the "Power of One," instead of the power of many devices. You still have *one* set of weapons, but they can span many virtual locations and options.

There are also some features that apps have that paper does not, like the ability to search, prioritize, or sort. Paper solutions just do not have these abilities.

Yet, if you are more comfortable with a paper list or a physical calendar, it still might be better to choose a day planner. As always, make your selection based on what you will actually use in your day-to-day.

Still confused? Again, it really doesn't matter as long as you have only one of each of the four essential time management weapons at hand. Go for simplicity and go for tools that you enjoy using.

In our next few rules, we will look at each of the time management weapons in depth.

Ninja Wisdom

✖ There are four productivity tools that everyone needs: a to-do list, a calendar, address book, and a notebook.

✖ It doesn't matter *which* type of tools you use, as much as it is crucial to have the *right* set of tools.

✖ You only should have one of each kind of tool. Keep it to the minimum.

✖ Always choose tools you enjoy and will actually use regularly.

✖ Keep it simple. The best system is usually the simplest. Avoid overly complicated tools or devices, especially ones that you are not comfortable integrating into your daily life.

Ninja Training

Now that you know the vital time management weapons let's take an inventory.

Questions:

✖ Do you have a to-do list, calendar, address book, and notebook?

✖ Which (if any) are you missing?

✖ Do you have multiple of any? Can you consolidate?

✖ Which tools do you like or dislike using? Why?

Having the right tools is just the start. Now, let's look at how to use them effectively.

36

TOO MANY TIME-WEAPONS

I asked a coaching client to bring all of his time management weapons to our first meeting. "Everything?" he said.

He showed up with a tabletop full of stuff. Multiple lists, pads of paper, his phone, even a full-size desktop calendar. He must have had almost a dozen tools in all!

One of the first things he said was, "I don't know how I keep up with all of these!" then he laughed and added, "I guess that's part of the trouble!"

He had about *four* different to-do lists. Personal, work, and family calendars. And his contacts were scattered across three addresses books including a desktop box of business cards. We discussed how many productivity apps would allow him to merge these separate calendars and contacts into one source and color-code them from where they came from.

A long afternoon later, we had consolidated his tools so that he was using only one of each tool. This meant combining his tasks lists, merging his address books, and more. He created one to-do list to encompass all his work and collated his contacts into a single contact list on his phone. Finally, he added all of his calendars to one app and color-coded them by their area of responsibility.

When we were done, he had a *much* simpler set of tools that was infinitely more accessible and best suited to his personality and needs.

TOOLS OR TOYS?

When it comes to shiny gadgets, it can be hard to tell the difference between tools and toys.

For many of us, we are drawn to the magical electronic tools that allow us to work almost anywhere. But they can also be a significant source of distraction, interruption, and stress.

Take your phone, for example. Wikipedia and YouTube are just two of the millions of sources that give every internet user the wealth of human knowledge. But that same technology also tempts you with wasted time, games, and distractions. Remember that experiment from earlier? Your device will interrupt your life more often than a young child. Unlike a little kid, though, it won't ever grow out of it!

When it comes to your time management, you have to ask yourself, are your gadgets helping you get more done? Or are they actually, taking more of your time and attention?

Just because a device has great potential for productivity, is also has great potential for distraction.

If your gadgets are running your time for ruin, you might want to consider using a paper-based system. Despite all of the promises of an app, a paper-based system used religiously will beat the latest gadgets.

So, take a hard look at your tools and ask yourself if you are genuinely benefitting from them or whether they are just toys.

YOUR TO-DO LIST SHOULD

BE YOUR BEST FRIEND

*When your to-do list reminds you of a task you
forgot, you know it's working.*

"Can you show me your list?"

This question causes stress in many people.

"Of course, I have a list. Let me find it." Maybe they do have a rough list. Or perhaps, they produce multiple lists. One on paper. One test on their phone, and yet another on a random Post-it Note. Just writing that stresses me out.

Studies show that only thirteen percent of people actively keep a to-do list every day.

Do you have one? Well, are you actively using it?

That is the first question that I ask those wanting to improve their time management. After all, if you're going to get more done, you need to know what you need to accomplish. And that's where your list comes in.

This one question usually separates those who are trying to improve versus those that "want" to.

If you could only have one time management tool at your disposal, it would have to be a good to-do list.

Your to-do list's one job is to track your tasks so that your brain doesn't have to. Instead of trying to remember every last thing you need to do, you can free your head space up so that it can concentrate on actually getting your work done.

The Most Powerful Productivity Weapon

A to-do list is the most important time management tool at your disposal. A list of all the tasks you want to track gets you going, lets you know what you need to do, and helps you prioritize your work. It can be a paper-based list (some people like to use day planners or craft their own Bullet Journal in a blank notebook). Or it can be an app on your phone that syncs across all your platforms.

A good to-do list will let you sort your to-dos by area of responsibility (work or personal) and order them by priority. Of course, you can do this all by hand on paper if you so choose. The purpose of your list should be tracking all of your work, which also allows you to see your progress. How good it feels to cross something off!

This sounds like a win all the way around. Yet, there's that looming statistic. Eighty-seven percent of people aren't regularly using this simple and essential tool.

The key factor here is to use it every single day.

You simply can't afford to make a list only when you feel like it. You need to have a list that continuously tracks your work and obligations.

Like a good friend, your to-do list should always have your back. It's a unique friend, too. It's always available, always precise, and will always remember your tasks, so you don't have to.

Actually, you should never *not* be keeping a list. I have witnessed people who start a new list each day. This is a dangerous way to live because you lose everything that was on the list the day before. It's like living your life as a "do

41

over" every single day. Just because you go to sleep doesn't mean the tasks reset or go away.

Don't Resist Your List

One of the excuses I hear from those who don't maintain a list is that they will "remember" their tasks later. Unfortunately, you won't remember, and then you will inevitably get burned by the forgotten item.

Our brains aren't designed to remember dozens of tasks. Studies have shown that our "working memory" is limited to about four active items at one time. This isn't practical when you want to track many to-dos at once. If you are trying to "keep it all in your head" you are wasting valuable memory and brainpower that you could dedicate to the work you are doing.

Others are afraid that if they write it down, they must do it later. This is silly. It's your list, and you can add, change, or delete things (those that turn out to be unimportant) at any time. Just because you put it in your list doesn't mean you are obligated to do it.

It's better to capture a to-do and delete it later, rather than miss a potentially important task.

When You Think of It, Put It on Your List

People often ask what kinds of tasks they should put on their list. "Should I add all tasks? Or just the most important ones?"

The answer is yes. You should add all the tasks to your list, no matter how big or how small. No matter how important or trivial. Everything that you may need to do now or in the future. Your list is there to remember your work, so you don't have to.

So, when you think of an item, don't wait until later. Immediately pull out your list and add it. This should only take a few seconds, but it requires discipline to do this every time you think of a task.

What Should You Be Doing Right Now?

When it comes to being more productive, one of the key questions to ask yourself is, "What should I be doing right now?"

This is where your list has your back. When you don't know what you should be doing, you need to look at your to-dos.

Your list is there to remind you of what you need to do and identify which tasks are most important. So, your list shouldn't be disposable. If you are writing lists on Post-it Notes or pads, that get lost or misplaced, you are going to lose tasks.

Rather than having those to-dos in random places, add them to your *one* list. This will ensure that you have all of your obligations in one place. Your to-do list should be a continuous list that is always tracking what you might need to do next.

Your Menu of Productivity

Your to-do list is a "productivity menu." It shows you all the options, items, and priorities that are available for your time.

When you complete a to-do and are ready to start a new one, make sure you review your list. Don't just pick up whatever is in front of you or at the top of your email inbox. If you do, you will be busy, but not doing your most important work.

Take a moment to regroup and collect your thoughts. This prevents you from being reactionary and simply jumping on whatever task happens to be in front of you. A good practice is to stop and consult your list. Review what you have completed and what the next priority is. Your list is your "menu" of what you need to do next.

In other words, if it's not on your list, don't do it.

Prioritize Your List (and Your Life)

Keeping a list is an excellent first effort. However, having an enormous list of things to do is only the first step. You need to order them by degree of importance.

If you don't prioritize your list, you will likely choose to-dos that are easy, but not significant. Your to-do list allows you to put your tasks in order of how important they are to your efforts.

44

If you are using a paper list, you can use priority labels like "A, B, C..." or "1, 2, 3..." However, a good highlighter or two is usually more effective and quicker.

This is an area where an app-based to-do list shines. You can order your items without having to rewrite your list. Most apps can show you a subset of your current or most essential tasks.

One List to Rule Them All

Before you get "list happy," it is important to note that you want to maintain *one* list as described in the "Power of One."

A common mistake is to have multiple lists for home, work, etc. The problem that arises is that you end up with different lists that are separated or out-of-sync. This makes it more difficult to compare your priorities and to get an overview of all your workload at once.

As mentioned in Tip 2, you should have "one list." It can be a master list that has sub-lists within it. I say you should keep one list that encompasses all aspects of your life.

Having one list may seem overwhelming if it is a large collection of tasks. However, the benefits of keeping all your work in one known place is *powerful*. To-do apps again shine here because they give the power and flexibility to create near endless list of tasks and sub-sections.

Regardless of whether you use paper or an electronic solution you want to be able to pare down the view of your list to what you need to do today. I call this your "Today List." Many apps allow you to do this as a feature, or by task due date. This allows you to look at the subset of to-dos that you want to complete today.

If you are using a paper list, you can use highlighters or separate pages to identify your "today items."

May the List Be with You, Always

For your to-do list to help you become a time ninja, it needs to be with you at all times. Yes, *at all times*. It doesn't matter if you are working, socializing, or whatever. Your to-do list needs to be ready to capture ideas, tasks, and more.

This is why I recommend that most people utilize an app for their to-do list. I am not trying to talk you out of a paper-based list. They have many positive traits. However, almost everyone carries their phone with them at all times.

The downside of an app-based list is that is lives in your phone, which means that it is not visible when your phone is off. Out of sight can mean out of mind. And as mentioned before, picking up your phone can lead to much time wasting without discipline.

You never know when you will think of something you need to do, and your list needs to be on-hand to capture that task. You may be out to dinner or at a work event or even at your kid's sports game, and when that idea happens make sure you write it down on your list right then and there.

The bottom line is that you want to keep your list close and let it fulfill its duty—track all of your tasks. If it's not with you and readily available, you won't be able to capture those fleeting tasks when they happen.

As a time management ninja, your to-do list will be your friend when distraction and overwhelm are on the prowl.

Ninja Wisdom

✖ Your to-do list should remember tasks so you can concentrate on your work.

✖ Keep one list and prioritize it to ensure you work on the most critical tasks.

✖ Capture all tasks big and small when they arise.

✖ Ensure your list is always with you.

Ninja Training

Now that we have discussed the power and habits of a productive to-do list, look at your list now and review it using the following questions:

✖ What type of a list do you use? Paper or app?

✖ Do you have more than one list? If you have more than one list, are you finding that it to be productive, or are there many tasks that are being left by the wayside?

✖ Do you prioritize your list(s)? If not, order your list. Rank your tasks by importance using a numbering or lettering system.

✖ Do you carry your list with you at all times?

THE BLANK SLATE

Once upon a time, I had a manager reporting to me who would start every day fresh. I mean this literally (in this stationery sense, of course).

This individual chose to keep their to-do list on a yellow legal pad. A very good choice, especially because this person kept this pad with them at all times.

So far, pretty good to-do list habits.

So, where did this person go wrong?

Each day this individual would come into my office and ask, "What do you need me to do today?" While he was saying this, he would rip the top few sheets off the yellow legal pad.

One day, I asked bluntly, "What about all the tasks on those pages you just threw away?"

He nonchalantly said, "Oh. Those were yesterday's tasks."

I was shocked to learn that he started every day with a blank slate of a to-do list. There was no follow-through, accountability, or continuity to his task list. If it didn't get done in a day, it was discarded and forgotten.

I was suddenly aware of why this manager had a reputation of forgetfulness and not being counted on by his peers to get the job done.

He was literally and intentionally erasing his to-do list each day. While this may sound like a fun way to live (or the plot of a comedy movie), it is not a productive way to work. Your list should always be continuous. It never gets to completion because it is a living document. It is a running record that runs day-to-day and week-to-week and, well, you get the point.

Don't let yourself fall victim to the "blank slate" mindset.

TIP 4

MAKE APPOINTMENTS

WITH YOURSELF AND

YOUR WORK

*Don't be afraid of your calendar. Own
your own schedule.*

Most people keep a calendar. It's what tells you where you need to be and when. If you take a closer look at it, most meetings on it are probably other people's stuff.

Meetings you must attend. Events you must remember. Obligations to which you said yes.

Does your calendar reflect what you need to do? Or are you guilty of filling up your schedule with everyone else's priorities?

Make Appointments with Yourself

I always find it interesting that what is on most people's calendars are activities they need to do for others.

If you work in a corporate workplace, you are probably familiar with this phenomenon. Your schedule fills up with meetings to the point where it looks like a Tetris board.

To take back control of your time, you *need* to take control of your calendar. Always remember, it's your time first. Too often I see individuals' calendars that are merely a list of other people's priorities and work.

Make sure you use your calendar to schedule for yourself and your priorities. How can you do this?

Block Your Time

The best way to control what's on your calendar is to fill it up before others do. I call this, "Blocking your time."

Before the week starts, (two weeks in advance would be even better), block out time on your calendar. This means scheduling time for yourself and *your* work.

Some people feel uncomfortable with this practice at first. You may even feel selfish about blocking out your calendar in large blocks. But that is precisely what you should do.

You need to flip the model. Instead, of squeezing in your essential work between other people's requests, make them schedule around your calendar.

How do you do this? You need to make appointments with yourself and with your work. Yes, you should schedule meetings with your most important tasks. Only when you block time for your personal projects, you will allocate adequate time for them.

Your calendar should be for your work and appointments first before you add requests from others.

There is a time etiquette angle here. It is hard to say no to requests for your time when you don't have that time allocated.

However, it is much easier to tell yourself and others, "Sorry, I am busy at that time."

You will be surprised by how quickly you can take back control of your time and calendar. After only a week or two of blocking your time, you will find a drastic change in the way your time is spent.

Don't Be Afraid to Fill Up Your Calendar

You may be nervous about filling up your calendar. You think that if you do, you will be too busy and your day will be too hectic.

This is only true if your calendar is overloaded with others' requests.

When you fill your calendar with your priorities and work, you will find that you have less hectic days and less stress in your activities. You'll have more time allocated for what matters.

Similarly to what we said about to-do lists, you may also think that if you put something on your calendar that you must do it. When you control your calendar and time, it is effortless to change the appointments that you made with yourself. (You only have to check with one person!)

So, don't be afraid to fill your calendar right on up!

Most people let their calendar fill up with meetings, invites, and other obligations and *then* try to fit their priorities in the space in-between. The point is to fill up your calendar first with the important items. And then let the non-important stuff fill in the time between.

What can you put on your calendar? Anything that is important to you.

Here are just a few examples of things you should be putting on your calendar:

- ✦ Personal appointments

- ✦ Workout time (whether it's at the gym or going for a run)

✦ Hobbies

✦ Time for your goals

✦ Sleep

✦ Meditation time

✦ Cleanup activities

✦ Time to spend with your family and friends

✦ "Me" time

Practice the "Right to Decline"

In addition to the blocks and self-made appointments on your calendar, you will also have meetings from others. As mentioned, it's important to remember that these should be secondary to your work.

In addition to filling up your calendar before others do, you need to be able to say no to requests when appropriate. Just because someone sent you an invite does not mean that you have to accept.

It doesn't matter if it is a birthday party, a date, or a work meeting—you should be able to decline if it makes more sense for you.

Too often, you will feel obligated to say yes just because you got a request for your time. This can be particularly true in work environments. As always, it is important to strike a balance. You don't want to end up regretting an all-nighter. All with moderation.

The Rise of Digital Calendars

Stats show that up to seventy percent of adults rely on digital calendars. Likely, it's because their job already uses Outlook or Google Calendar. Digital calendars are easy to access with your phone and always have your appointments with you. Digital calendars can also provide reminders and other pertinent information about your upcoming appointments. A paper calendar isn't going to buzz and remind you that you are late to your next obligation.

Perhaps the biggest advantage of digital calendars is that they are "cloud-based" and can be synced, shared, and viewed across multiple platforms. You can share your calendar with others, view it on your desktop computer, and never worry about missing appointments that were written down on another calendar.

Ninja Wisdom

✖ Make appointments with yourself and your work.

✖ Block time on your calendar before other people fill it up.

✖ Don't be afraid to fill it up. You will have more productivity if it is filled with your activities.

✖ Just because you got an invite to a meeting doesn't mean you have to say yes.

Ninja Training

Take a few minutes to review your calendar by asking yourself the following:

✖ Is it filled with your priorities or with other people's requests and obligations?

✖ Which appointments on your calendar could/should you have declined? Can you still decline them? (Good thumb rule is yes, if they are more than twenty-four hours away)

✖ Block your calendar for the next two weeks. Make appointments for your work, goals, and priorities.

HAVE A FAMILY CALENDAR

We discussed many of the benefits of having a digital calendar. While many people use a shared calendar at work, far fewer utilize the technology in the personal lives. Many families struggle with the tech behind sharing calendars that will let them know what the family is up to and when.

It does not have to be difficult! Having a shared family (or friends) calendar can help you stay organized in your personal life. It avoids confusion amongst family members and sets up positive expectations about when and where people need to be. Compare this to the last-minute chaos that many families live day-today trying to juggle the myriad obligations of family members.

Here are just a few of the things you probably want on your shared family calendar:

✘ Kid's school events

✘ Work events that impact the family

✘ Dinner dates for Mom and Dad

✘ Fun events for the family

✘ Kid's sports and activities

✘ Travel and vacation

WRITE IT DOWN NOW,

SO YOU DON'T HAVE TO

REMEMBER IT LATER

Let your notes remember so that your brain doesn't have to.

Have you ever had to go searching for a piece of information only to waste an excessive amount of time looking for it?

It could be a phone number, a receipt, or even a meeting note from a few years ago.

You would think that in our internet-based world we would have all the information we need at our fingertips. Yet, even the best search engine can't help you find the personal information that you are seeking. If only...

Taking notes sounds like such a school-driven activity. In fact, many people stop taking notes once they're out of school. Yet, note-taking is a skill that can serve you in all areas of your life. At work, at home, and even in your hobbies and leisure.

The simple fact is that, while wondrous machines, our brains are not skilled at keeping lots of miscellaneous information readily available.

Our brains are limited in both the capacity and duration of short-term memory. That is why you cannot recall a new person's name after you meet them, or the numbers from yesterday's meeting.

Strangely, have you ever recalled the lyrics from a song from years ago but not remembered the room number of the hotel you checked into a few hours ago?

Let's explore how your notebook will make you more productive.

Write It Down...Before You Forget

When was the last time you took notes? Maybe in a meeting at work? Or in a class or hobby in your spare time?

Taking notes is a magical activity. Not only does it give you a record of information to refer to later, but research shows that just *writing* it helps you recall the information that you documented in the first place. Physically jotting it down helps transition information from short-term to long-term memory. The repetition of writing and reviewing notes is powerful for retention of information.

It's that simple. Write it down now, so you don't have to remember it later.

However, for the purposes of effectively planning your time, the main reason to write things down is so that you don't have to remember them. By writing down notes, you have a permanent record that you can refer back to (far more efficient than searching your memory).

Of course, the next question is, "Where are you keeping your notes?"

One Place for Your Notes

As we discussed earlier, you need to have a notebook in which to capture your notes. You should have *one place* for all your notes.

However, writing it down is only half the battle. If you can't find that information again when it is needed, it does you no good to write it down in the first place.

One of the pitfalls of note-taking that many fall into is that they take notes in too many places. In fact, a notebook is the tool most likely missing from most people's toolbox.

If you are like most, you have notes located in multiple places. Perhaps, in a composition notebook, a loose-leaf sheet of paper, or a pad of paper.

It always amazes me how many sources of loose papers and notebooks people find—an extra legal pad, the little-bound notebooks that many conferences give out, a Post-it, and even the proverbial "back of a napkin."

Yet, when taking notes in many places, you are complicating your ability to keep track of them. As with your to-do list, calendar, and address book, I recommend that you keep a single notebook, or maybe one notes "solution."

You may be concerned about keeping all your notes in one place, but the benefits outweigh the negatives. You can easily keep a notebook with multiple sections or sub-notebooks, which is very easy to do with paper *and* apps.

Paper vs. Electronic Notes

Which is the better medium for your notes, paper or technology?

Again, choose what suits you. (See Tip 2, and "Choose the Weapons You'll Actually Use.") If you are better at taking notes in one versus the other, then, by all means, use the solution that works for you.

However, the argument for an electronic solution is very compelling for your notebook. Having your notes in an electronic format allows you to have all your genius ideas with you at all times.

I have shelves of written notebooks that I took years ago, before mobile devices. While there is good information contained in them, those scribbles are not very useful, portable, or searchable.

Imagine being able to recall your notes anyplace and anytime. That is the power of a central electronic note-taking solution. There are many great solutions out there, like Apple Notes, Evernote, OneNote, Daylite, and more. Most of these are searchable by a variety of methods including keywords, hashtags, location (where you took the note), and even by handwriting recognition for written, photographed notes. Incredible!

I was in a meeting one day, and a conversation came up about a contract discussion that had taken place several years prior.

While other participants were debating what "they remembered" to be the terms of the previous agreement, I quickly opened up my notes app and searched for the meeting notes.

To everyone's surprise except my own, I found the exact notes from a discussion six years prior. Within moments, I was displaying and quoting from the original meeting notes regarding the topic at hand.

Not only were people amazed, but they were also stunned into silence. Time ninja moves stun anyone.

What Should You Put in Your Notes?
(Hint: Everything)

If you think there is a chance you will need something in the future, then capture it in your notes.

Write it down now, so you don't have to remember it in the future.

Can you take too many notes? Sure you can. You don't need to capture every conversation word-for-word. That would be an effort in insanity, and it would drive those around you crazy. I have seen this behavior from an individual who typed so much on their laptop that they weren't even absorbing the conversation.

However, there are many things you can "capture" beyond the traditional handwritten notes.

Here are just a few suggestions of what else you can capture:

- ✦ **Solutions to problems:** If you have ever found yourself solving the same question more than once, then make sure you save that information.

- ✦ **Personal information:** This can include individual and family information about clothing sizes, cars, ID numbers, and more.

- ✦ **Reference data:** It is much easier to order maintenance items if you have the model/reference numbers of batteries, lightbulbs, etc.

- ✦ **Pictures:** A picture is often the quickest way to capture the current state of something.

- **Receipts:** For large or important purchases, capture your receipts into your notebook, so you have them whether now or years from now.

- **Whiteboards:** When in meetings, pay attention to the conversation and participate. You can take a picture of the whiteboard with your device after the meeting.

- **Documents:** Your notebook isn't intended as a filing system. But you should capture copies of important reference documents that you may need at a future time.

Take a Picture, It's Worth a Thousand Notes

Visual note-taking is a literal thing. With technology, you (well, your computer) can have a photographic memory. Just a few years ago, we didn't have this ability, but our smartphones are wonderful tools. Now that we all carry electronic devices on our person and can take almost limitless amounts of pictures, they deserve a special mention.

We have our smartphones with us 24/7/365. Remember how phones are like affairs? Most people sleep with their phones right next to them. (More on that in a later chapter.)

Some great ideas of things to take pictures of:

- Signs or store hours that are not easy to locate on the internet.

- The room number of your hotel room.

✦ Where you parked your car (yes, some cars now track this, but this is still easier).

✦ Papers or documents. Sometimes you don't need to scan a doc or flyer. Just a quick picture will do the job.

✦ Items that you might want to buy in a store.

✦ The physical solution to a problem. How did that look before you took it apart?

Ninja Wisdom

- ✖ Taking notes has the dual benefits of keeping a record, as well as improving your own memory.

- ✖ If you think there is even a *remote chance* you may need it later, write it down now.

- ✖ Even more than with the previous tools, consider the benefits of an electronic-based notebook solution. The ability to search years' worth of information instantly makes it a compelling solution.

- ✖ Don't limit your notebook directly to ideas, thoughts, and points you write down. Capture pictures, solutions, and more.

- ✖ It may be a misnomer to say, "one notebook," but you need one place to keep your notes so that you have one place to look for them later. You can have sub-notebooks and journals but keep a "solution" for all your note-based cataloging.

Ninja Training

Most people can use some help with their notebook. Let's make sure you have one place to keep your notes and look at what you could be capturing.

✘ What is your one notebook? If you have more than one notebook, does that method help you remember and later find important information?

✘ Do you use an electronic solution? If not, should you consider a smartphone or cloud-based note-taking app?

✘ What do you capture today in your notebook?

✘ What other things could you be capturing in your notebook? Think about the solutions that you have had to solve multiple times. Or information that you repeatedly look up.

THE BENEFITS OF AN ELECTRONIC NOTEBOOK

If you were going to use technology for only one of your time management weapons, your notebook would probably be your best bet.

Many people resist taking notes electronically. It is often still easier to jot things down with a pen or pencil. But in many cases, those notes are taken in random places such as random pads of paper or Post-its.

If you are disciplined about keeping your notes in an app-based solution, there are many benefits:

✘ **Search:** The most significant advantage is the ability to search *all* of your notes instantly. This just isn't possible with a Moleskine or other paper-based notebook.

✘ **Sync:** If you use one app, you can get to your notes no matter what device you are on: mobile, desktop, or even the web.

✘ **Backup:** I once lost a notebook on the road that I left on the top of my truck. My notes literally blew away in the wind. Electronic notes can be backed up regularly to protect against loss.

✘ **Portability:** Your notes can be with you everywhere, especially on your phone. Again, this doesn't work with multiple volumes of paper notebooks.

PLANNING IS GOOD,

PREPARING IS

EVEN BETTER

*Having a plan is essential to having a
successful day.*

Do you have a plan before you leave the house in the morning?

Most people don't. They head into their day without a plan or schedule. Without knowing what they need to do, where they need to be, and even where they want to go.

These are the individuals in the office that are at the coffee machine for the third time before they even start working. They don't have an urgency to begin their day, and most of the time they don't even know what they should be doing.

I am always amazed by how many people rush into their day without a thought (or care) about what they need or want to accomplish. At the end of their day, how do they know if they were successful?

Without a plan, you are just miming your way through your day.

Have a Plan Every Day

There are two main reasons that people avoid planning their day.

They either fall into the "I don't have time to plan" category, or they tell themselves that having a plan is "too restrictive." They want to go with the flow and be free with their day.

Both of these excuses couldn't be more misdirected.

You *do* have time to plan your day. As we discussed in Tip 1, when you are more efficient with your time, you will have more time. You will actually *save* time by investing the few minutes required to plan. Instead of being reactive to things thrown your way and doing tasks in a panic, you go in with a purpose and mission.

Secondly, planning your day doesn't mean you are locked down to a restrictive agenda. Instead, it frees your mind up to concentrate on what's essential, while letting your day follow the best path possible.

Managing your time is never meant to be limiting. Instead, you should see it as a way to expand your time. Having a plan for your day gives you a sense of purpose and can help you relax. Yes, you finally know what you need to do today and how/when you are going to do it.

It's *your* plan. You can adapt and change course as life requires. You only have to check with yourself before changing it.

Make a Plan *Before* You Start Your Day

Making a daily plan is not difficult. It should only take about five minutes, and no more than ten.

And yes, you *definitely* have five to ten minutes to plan your day. Plus, being productive can end up saving hours. What are you waiting for?

Here are the simple steps to plan your day:

- ✦ **Review your calendar:** Where do you need to be and when today? Are there any meetings you need to verify or cancel in advance?

- ✦ **Review your to-do list:** What do you need to do today? Which are the most important priorities on your list?

↗ **Review your notes from the day before:** Is there any information that you captured yesterday that needs to be added to your schedule or to-do list?

That's it. You are now more organized than ninety percent of the people starting their day.

Managing your day helps avoid surprises. It avoids forgotten meetings and prevents you from forgetting the items at home that you need during your day. Now, you know what you need and want to do and when you want to do them. Efficiently planning and reducing effort by taking five minutes to plan your day will definitely give you back hours.

Now that you have a plan, it's time to prepare to carry it out.

Planning Is Good, Preparing Is Better

Planning is good, but there is more.

Know what you need to do and when is the foundation that lets you operate from a position of efficiency.

The next step is to actually *prepare* for your day.

Preparing is the act of actually getting ready to do the things on your schedule and to-do list. It means gathering the materials that you will need with you to perform a specific task on your list. It can mean preparing for a meeting. Doing the pre-work before an event.

Preparing ensures you are ready to carry out your plan, which will multiply your plan's effectiveness tenfold. If you prepare for your plan, you will be ready to execute your day with less effort and more efficiency. This gets you ready and gives you time to review, do advance work, remedy any oversights or issues, and adapt.

Here is a simple set of steps to prepare for your day:

+ **Pack needed items:** Gather items that you will need to complete your tasks. This may include paperwork, reference materials, and more.

+ **Schedule time for your work:** As we learned in Tip 3, fill your calendar to block out time for your work.

+ **Do any required pre-work:** This step can be magical. Not many people actually do the homework needed to be ready for their day. It doesn't matter if you are a professional, student, or stay-at-home parent, doing the homework makes you prepared to tackle your day with ease.

When you do the advance preparation for your day, you are that much more ready to be successful.

Ninja Wisdom

- ✖ Have a plan before you start each day.

- ✖ It only takes a few minutes to come up with a plan that could save you hours later.

- ✖ Planning is first, and then preparing can make you even more ready to take on the day.

Ninja Training

Take a moment to map out the path of your day. You can make a blueprint for today, or even tomorrow if today is almost over. Then look at what prep work you can do in advance.

Make a plan:

- ✖ What appointments are on your calendar today?

- ✖ What tasks on your to-do list do you need to complete today?

- ✖ Prepare for your day:

- ✖ What do you need to pack for your activities today?

- ✖ What homework can you do in advance of the day?

DO YOUR "HOMEWORK"

Preparing for your day is essentially "doing the homework" before your day begins. Sorry for those who thought that homework ended once you left school...

Too many people don't prepare in advance and then stumble through their day's activities. Imagine how much easier your day would be if you took a few minutes to prepare for each event on your schedule.

Here are just a few examples of how you can prepare for your day:

- ✗ **Pack your lunch:** Avoid getting so busy at work that you skip lunch.

- ✗ **Do the reading for your meetings:** Read the advance materials in *advance*. You will be the smartest person in the room.

- ✗ **Pack your belongings for the day:** Make sure to include any items needed for tasks or appointments.

- ✗ **Confirm appointments:** A quick email or text confirmation could prevent wasting time on cancelled or forgotten meetings by others.

- ✗ **Review your inbox:** Make sure there are no last-minute messages you need to know about before starting your day.

BE THE EARLY BIRD AND

GET A HEAD START ON

THE WORLD

The early bird is secretly a ninja: it gets a head start while everyone else is still sleeping.

What time did you get up today?

Did you get an early start, or did you get up at the very last minute before you had to run out the door?

Getting an early start to your day can make all the difference between a successful day and one that ends up in chaos. When you get up early, you get a head start on your priorities and work.

That way, when you get the wheels turning on your actual duties (be it a day that starts with taking the kids to school or going to work) you are already a step ahead of everyone else.

You may be saying, "Sounds great, but I can't get up that early." But no one is born with an innate inability to wake up early.

Being an early bird is a choice.

The Secrets of the Early Bird

There is a secret among the early birds. They've kindly passed it on to all time management ninjas.

The secret is that ultra-productive people get more done in the morning before most people even get up. Some studies have shown that 90 percent of top-level executives wake up before six. They are often up before the sun, getting their priorities done before the chaos of their day has a chance to rear its ugly head. Getting up early gives you a head start on the world.

What time did I get up this morning? Four o'clock. I do almost every morning.

Yes, you probably recoiled. Most people do. Then, they accuse me of either not sleeping or having special abilities.

How did I acquire this superpower?

Well, it's more of a habit than a superpower. I learned to be an early bird via many years of practice. Many years of getting an early start to my day.

You, too, can learn to be an early bird.

Making Excuses to Sleep In

I hear this excuse often: "I can't get up that early. That's crazy!"

The truth is you *can* get up that early. You just choose not to.

You make choices that prevent you from getting an early start. Maybe it is staying up too late. Or perhaps, you have let yourself get out of shape so that you don't have the energy.

The irony in this excuse is that getting up early actually *gives* you more energy. It builds momentum and provides a head start in all areas of your life.

Why *wouldn't* you want to get a head start each and every day?

Have a Purpose and a Routine

It's important to note that getting up early only works if you actually do something productive with that morning time.

If you get up early and merely read the news, check your email, and surf the internet, then you are just shifting non-productive activities to your morning. That is just as bad as staying up late doing the same.

Instead, you need a morning routine.

The morning hours are often called magical. They are quiet. They are usually free from interruptions, other people, and communication. You can get peace, all for yourself.

What could you get done with a couple hours of quiet, uninterrupted time?

You could work out. Work on your goals. Write. Meditate. Work on a degree. Read or study. *Whatever is important to you.* You can also take a few minutes to plan and prepare for your day. All before the day begins.

Here is my sample routine:

>   4 a.m. Get up

>   4–5 a.m. Writing and planning/preparing for my day

>   5–6 a.m. Workout at the gym

>   6–7 a.m. Get kids ready for school

>   7–8 a.m. Continue planning and preparing for my day

>   8:15 a.m. Ready to start my workday!

Sounds terrific, doesn't it?

> *By the time most people are rushing to get to work by nine o'clock, I have already accomplished some of my most important work and activities of the day.*

Get Up Just a Little Earlier

If you aren't currently an early bird, then getting up at four o'clock may sound crazy! However, you don't have to change your sleep schedule overnight to become an early bird.

If getting up early doesn't sound appealing to you, I recommend you try getting up just twenty minutes earlier than you currently do. Even with that small increment you will start to see changes in your day. You won't be rushing out the door or late to work. You will have time to prepare for your day before starting your workday.

After that, try a half hour or more until you find that getting up earlier gives you enough time to do some important tasks before leaving the house. As mentioned, getting up early is only beneficial if you have intentional tasks to do during that time. So, as you start to reclaim the morning hours, start to detail your routine and what you want to do during that time.

As you transition to an early bird schedule, you will find that you start to wean yourself from staying up late. You may even realize that much of what you did at night was time wasted watching Netflix or surfing the internet.

You can choose to seize each day with ferocity. The day is your worm! Grab it before it's gone.

It's a great way to start the day!

Ninja Wisdom

✖ Scrambling for time? You can start your day early!

✖ Get your most important tasks done while others are still sleeping.

✖ Have a routine and be purposeful with your early hours.

✖ Begin your day with a sense of accomplishment and motivation.

Ninja Training

If you want to become an early bird, you will need to look at your current schedule and activities. Ask yourself:

✖ What are you doing at night that is taking away from sleep? Does it make you feel unproductive?

✖ What actions do you need to do differently? (i.e., go to bed early, cut out certain activities, change your routine.)

✖ What will it take for you to get up earlier?

✖ What is the time will you commit to setting your alarm for?

✖ What will you *do* with the early morning time that you will be gaining?

✖ Write a *detailed* routine for your morning hours.

- What do you do in the morning and when?

- Is your current routine helping you be more productive?

- What else could you benefit from doing *before* your day begins?

EARLY BIRDS VS. NIGHT OWL

There is a distant cousin to the early bird. And it is the night owl.

These are the individuals who burn the midnight oil versus getting up early.

There is nothing wrong with being a night owl. However, most people will find better success in getting up early. Not only does it give you a head start on your day, but it prevents interruptions and other urgencies from interrupting your most important work.

Being a night owl can be tough because you are trying to do some of your toughest work at the end of your day. You are most likely going to be tired from your day and thus not able to deliver your best work.

Again, some people swear by the night hours instead of dawn time. If you do go with a night routine, I still recommend setting a specific routine for your extra time. Just as with the early hours, staying up late and not accomplishing specific priorities isn't productive either.

DO TASKS UNTIL DONE

Undone tasks create more work. Procrastinating only means you'll have to put in more effort later.

Are you guilty of putting tasks down before they are completely done?

You get a to-do *almost* complete. And then, what do you do?

You stop. You pause *just* short of finishing the item at hand.

Then, before you realize it, you pick up the next interesting thing and tell yourself that the first task is almost done. So, that's good enough. Right?

Yet, it's not done. So, you either leave it partially done *or* you start multitasking.

Either way, you are creating more work for yourself. We'll explore how undone tasks actually take more effort to complete. Doing more than one task at once only leads to multiple tasks done at partial effort.

Unfinished Tasks Create More Work

When you don't finish a task and have to return to it at a later time, it takes *more* effort to complete it than if you had finished it the first time around.

If you don't have time to do it now, you're not going to have even more time to do it later.

The first step to starting something after procrastinating is picking up where you left off. Obviously, trying to figure *this* out takes up time. Then, there are what I call "penalties" for not completing the task.

Penalties can include:

↘ **Late fees:** These can be fines or additional costs when you do something late, after a deadline, or simply just in a rush. There are entire industries that make a living on tasks that were left to the last minute. (Think: FedEx, Amazon.)

↘ **Missed Opportunities:** Sometimes the penalty for putting something off is an opportunity that passes you by. A job that you didn't finish your application for. Something that you were going to purchase that is now sold out.

↘ **Task Rot:** Finally, penalties can be a result of what I like to call "task rot." The task you left undone is now rotten and requires additional time and effort to complete than if you had done it right away. For instance, when you stop paperwork tasks like filing papers or signing documents, you end up spending *extra* time trying to get back on track. Where exactly did I leave off? Where is that folder? Getting out of that task flow is pricey. Or it can be a physical task that requires more effort if left for later, like leaving dirty dishes in the sink overnight. Or, for a week! Sounds like a cesspool.

↘ **More Stress:** Thinking about undone work takes a toll on your mind and can prevent you from getting enough rest or sleep. Which means less energy for doing those undone tasks. Which means more stress. Negative feedback loop, anyone?

Multitasking Leads to Lesser Performance

Some people *think* they are good at multitasking.

"I can do *several* things at once!" they tell others.

Yet, multitasking never leads to good results or effective performance. Ever try to talk to someone while they are tapping away on their phone? That is called a one-sided conversation. Multitasking is not productive no matter what individuals want to brag about.

Multitasking divides your attention and cognitive abilities. Instead of giving your all to one activity, you are only able to produce sub-standard performance for several. In fact, data shows that most adults show a cognitive IQ drop of *fifteen points* when they are trying to do multiple tasks at the same time.

Is this the performance you want to be known for?

Sometimes multitasking is downright dangerous. Texting and driving is a classic example of this in action. Heck, even texting and *walking* for some people. I can't be the only one who's hit a few poles.

You may *think* you are dividing your attention and getting more things done. However, research has proven that you would be better off doing them serially (one after the other) rather than at the same time.

The human mind isn't good at doing multiple things at the same time. Multitasking just means you are doing more with less quality.

Get to "Done"

Most people struggle *immensely* when trying to continue doing a task to completion. Here's how it goes—they begin a to-do, do most of it, and then move on to another task. Meanwhile, the task left behind is left utterly incomplete.

Sound familiar? Multitasking can be a direct cause of tasks not being completed. You end up with several things started and *nothing* finished. Needless to say, this is *not* a productive way to work. No wonder when the end of the day comes, you are exhausted, and yet have accomplished, well, *nothing*.

Resist the nearly irresistible temptation to let interruptions take you off task. Best way? *Don't* start a second task until you have finished the one at hand. This requires a lot of discipline and focus. Try setting a timer for ten minutes of complete focus. Once you're in that "flow," ten minutes will seem like nothing. Soon it'll be fifteen, thirty, an *hour* of total concentration.

You will find that when you go through a few important tasks completely, you will naturally outperform the many tasks that you started but didn't finish. Focus and *stay on task!*

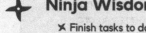

Ninja Wisdom

- ✖ Finish tasks to done.

- ✖ When you leave tasks uncompleted, they create more work for later.

- ✖ Undone tasks can incur penalties and other life consequences.

- ✖ Multitasking only leads to more work started at lesser quality.

Ninja Training

Addressing your tasks can be overwhelming. The best way to start is by scrutinizing your habits to see how you can best concentrate on finishing tasks to done. Maybe these can help you get started:

- ✖ Identify tasks that you often leave incomplete. (Laundry, expense reports, etc.) What have been some consequences of leaving tasks undone? A fight with your spouse? Spoiled food? Even coming in late to an appointment?

- ✖ Do you work on one task at a time or do you multitask? Do you start additional tasks while your original one is still in progress? What do you find usually happens?

- ✖ Name areas where you probably should be multitasking. Name areas that would benefit from one-on-one combat.

HOW TO GET TO "DONE"

If you are a chronic multitasker, you are probably familiar with neglected to-dos and projects. Here are six tips to aid you in dueling with your to-do list:

1. **Use a Today List**: Have a list of the things that you *must get done today*. It is usually best to keep it separate from your to-do list. Starting out, I recommend you limit yourself to only **three** items on your Today List. If you get nothing else done today, you will finish what is on your Today List. These are the tasks that will be shown no mercy.

2. **Have a clean workspace**: The power of a clean workspace is often underestimated. Multitaskers are infamous for having cluttered workspaces. But, they will tell you, "No, no it's an *organized mess*." Before you can give them an eye-roll, they say, "Of course, I know where everything is!" Unfortunately, that's a consoling lie. A clean workspace is essential to getting things to done. Take five minutes to clean up your area before starting important work. Doesn't that look and feel nice?

3. **Resist starting other tasks**: No matter how simple or short the task, make an extra effort to not start other to-dos before finishing what you are working on. Catch yourself putting something down in midstream. Take action accordingly.

4. **Avoid interruptions**: Research has shown that after even the *simplest* of interruptions—*ping!*—it can require fifteen minutes or more to get back on track. When you are working on your high-priority items, minimize your chance of interruptions. Find a quiet place to work. Go to your "Fortress of Solitude" if you must. Close your door if necessary. Do not answer calls. Your productive future is at stake.

5. **Slay distractions**: The web and email are probably the best examples of fatal distractions. How many times have you been in the middle of a task and then suddenly decided to Google "Why do elephants have such a great sense of smell?" Can't be just me. Twenty-three websites later, you're shoulders-deep in NASA astronaut interviews and realize you really should get back to your work. Shut off your internet connection if you need to. If you're particularly desperate, download Freedom or SelfControl. It'll block all access to your select list of websites. Reduce these temptations by eliminating them, if even for a short time. Becoming a ninja means sacrificing the things you love. You will be rewarded.

6. **Build momentum**: Finishing tasks gives you more energy. The euphoria from completing something will drive your productivity even *higher*. That is why it is so powerful to complete tasks first thing in the morning. It accelerates you all day long. Stealthy ninja style.

PUT IT AWAY NOW, AND

YOU'LL KNOW WHERE IT

IS LATER

"If I knew where I had it last, it wouldn't be lost."
—George Carlin

This scenario is familiar across millennia. You're in a pinch, and you can't find the *one item* you're missing. Running out the door (already late! arghhh!) and suddenly...a burst of wind. Absentmindedly you reach for the shotgun seat. No... You can't believe it. In a fit of rage, you make a U-turn, fling the doors open, and sprint into your room, throwing every wretched coat rack. There's only one explanation. Your jacket decided to run away. Or have you been getting dressed for that critical interview (your *one* shot at a promotion) and just can't find your clean pair of pants? You washed them *yesterday*!

But it doesn't end there. You've lost other things. Maybe it is the receipt for something you purchased last week. Or the gloves that you haven't worn since last winter.

What have you lost lately? And how much time did you waste looking for it?

Lost Time Looking for Lost Items

At some point recently, you probably spent an inordinate amount of time looking for a lost item.

And I mean a *lot* of time. Maybe a few hours. And if it's something essential? God forbid, your *phone*? Easily, a few hours become a few *days*.

Likely, you made an even bigger mess by tearing apart your house in search of the missing item.

Eventually, you gave up. Went out to buy another one. Or you lost the benefit of the item, like a coupon, rebate, or even a gift card. That's free money! *Lost!*

Okay. Enough despair.

As frustrating as misplaced items can be, you can overcome this challenge by incorporating some discipline into your organization. Read closely. The best way to prevent items from getting lost in the first place is to *put them away in the first place*.

What? Sounds like common sense?

Yet, how many times have you lost *that one umbrella* because you didn't return it to its rightful place? Or you left it someplace unfamiliar?

It seems like it should be easy to put things away when you are done with them. It sounds elementary, Watson. As easy as it sounds, however, doing this requires the discipline to stop what you are doing and return an item to where it belongs. But...where *does* it belong?

It is hard to put things where they belong, when they don't even have a home.

Everything Needs a Home

I am going to tell you one of the biggest organizing secrets that will change the way you treat your possessions.

If you put things where they belong, you will save time, effort, and stress in your life.

But, it becomes increasingly difficult to put something away if it doesn't have a place to go. I call this a place a *home*.

Each item you possess needs a home, a cozy place that it gets returned to when it's not in use. Many things in your home (like silverware, clothes, tools, and more) probably *do* have a home already. Good! That makes it easier to get started. Stealthy time-saving moves have to begin somewhere.

If you know where something is supposed to be, and you always put it away, then you know where it is for next time.

The question is, what *else* could you give a home to?

The more of your possessions that you designate a place for, the easier it becomes to just put them away rather than set them down anywhere. Without homes, they end up wandering around your residence like nomads. Look around. There are *definitely* things that end up wherever you last used them because they never had a home to go to. Adopt them!

Small things (think car keys, pens, earphones) are easy enough to lose. But have you ever misplaced a large item, like a vacuum cleaner or a maybe a step stool? It's ridiculous. They're enormous! *How* on earth could you lose something like that? Did it just disappear? Three hours later, you end up finding them in some random room where they were last used, but then long forgotten.

If you're reading this and thinking, "Okay, I would *never* lose my giant ceramic dog," that's an excellent sign. The future isn't so bleak, young ninja.

To avoid getting to *that* point (or, well, stop losing vacuum cleaners once and for all), I dare you to take stock of your belongings and assign each one of them a cozy home sweet home.

Here are just some items that you can create a home for within your home:

- ✦ **Light bulbs:** Light bulbs often end up in strange places. Don't store them near the individual lamp (you likely have too many lamps to do this!), but rather in a central storage bin, so you always know where to find them.

- ✦ **Batteries:** Create a battery drawer to hold common batteries for home use. Stock up and label them! Be sure to dispose of used ones the moment they run out so you won't have to worry about trying a few hundred ones out.

- ✦ **Laundry baskets:** Yes, even your baskets should find their home in a good laundry room area. They should *only* be used for transporting and folding clothes, not (!) for storing them.

✦ **Medicines and medical supplies:** Create sick boxes for illness remedies and first aid boxes for cuts and bruises to containerize (yes, that's a word) your supplies. No more scouring through junk drawers with one hand while the other bleeds profusely. *Yikes.*

✦ **Flashlights:** Do you know where to find them when the power goes out? Tripping over rugs and furniture groping the dark for flashlights sounds perilous. Keep flashlights in a location that will be readily accessible in case the power goes out.

✦ **Umbrellas:** One of the best containers I recently bought was an umbrella basket. No more searching. Now, when it's already raining, everyone in the family knows where to go.

✦ **Gloves, mittens, hats:** How many times have you had to repurchase gloves and other winter items? Every house should have a glove-mittens-hats box in one of their hallway closets.

Becoming a time management ninja means streamlining your world. Here are just a few more organization ideas:

✦ **Clear storage boxes:** When it comes to making homes for your stuff, containers are great tools for grouping items together in one area. They provide a great way to capture like items together. Or items that share a specific purpose. Sewing kit? Shoeshine kit? *Umbrella bucket?* Don't limit yourself.

⁂ Key hooks: Set up a central set of key hooks near the main entrance of your home. No more scattered keys on countertops and in jacket pockets! They will *instantly* be at hand when you need them the most.

⁂ Drawers: Ensure that drawers are used for item homes—*not* used as landfills. Don't *ever* clear desks or countertops by swiping your arm across their surface and dumping the contents directly into the nearest drawer. (Yes, done that before. Still traumatized.) They are not trash chutes!

⁂ Closets: Closets are for *storage*, not piles. Finished closets are definitely worth the time, effort, and money—instead of a pile in your closet, have drawers, hanging space, and more *already set up for you*. These organization solutions are simple and will keep your closets *clean*. A quick organization check is to see if you can walk into your closet with ease. Is the floor clean or covered in stuff?

_____

What in your home needs a home?

_____

Ninja Wisdom

✖ Putting things away when you are done with them saves time looking for them later.

✖ Your possessions need a home so you always know where to find them.

✖ Containers are great ways to store supplies, kits, and more.

Ninja Training

What in your home needs a home?

✖ Look around your house. What are five things you could put away now? Ask yourself why they were left out in the first place. *Don't* take this as a guilt session. Instead, use this exercise to consider what you might do differently next time you use the item.

✖ Create three new homes for items in your home. What things can you think of that need a place to be put away? Don't know where to start? Consult the list above.

✖ Consider what similar items in your home could be centralized. Items that have multiple locations are excellent contenders. Just bring them together to *one* localized home. Again, the list above might help.

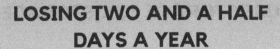

LOSING TWO AND A HALF DAYS A YEAR

We've been talking for a while now about losing items and losing time. However, it's really the time spent *looking* for those lost things that adds up. Studies have shown that the average adult spends ten minutes a day searching for items.

_____

If you spend just ten minutes a day searching, then you've lost over two and a half days a year.

_____

Two and a half days each year looking for lost stuff!!!

And of course, that doesn't count the time you spent three hours tearing your house apart looking for that *cursed mini fridge*. Can't be just me.

_____

Just think—if you put things away, how much time could you reclaim? What would you do with an extra two and a half days a year?

_____

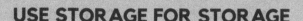

USE STORAGE FOR STORAGE

You would be surprised how many people cannot walk into their closets because it is filled to the brim with piles and stuff.

It's much easier to "put things away" if you actually have places to put them. But, it's hard to do that if your drawers, shelves, and such are not accessible.

Make sure that your storage solutions are used for just that...*storage*.

Are your drawers for storage? Or do you use them to hide things out of sight so that they are crammed with clutter that doesn't belong there? Didn't mean to call you out.

Here are just a few more examples:

✘ Laundry baskets are for carrying laundry, not storing it.

✘ Filing cabinets are for filing, not piles of unsorted papers.

✘ Storage containers made to help you organize items, not contain random things that you don't want to put away. Again, didn't mean to call you out.

THE ABC METHOD

OF CLEANING

The key to avoiding cleaning is to take care of clutter before it becomes a mess. Preemptive strikes

against clutter are always acceptable.

Is your life clean or is it full of clutter?

Last chapter we talked about putting things away to prevent them from being lost. Now, I want to discuss the act of cleaning as a way of preventing messes. Because when things are not put away, they are now *clutter*. And clutter quickly becomes a world of shambles that you have to clean up later. Not at all the way of the time ninja.

Here is the one-question quiz I ask people to gauge their overall clutter: *How clean is your car?*

Yes, a *lot* of people squirm when asked that question. Many people have junk in their trunk, be it sinewy running shoes, old shopping purchases, or just things that never made it into the house. If you have kids, I can almost *guarantee* that there is clutter in the back seat (old Goldfish crackers, crayons, and even Pokémon cards?). It's so terrifying that sometimes it seems better to never acknowledge it.

This question about vehicular cleanliness is a good overall indicator of the clutter in most people's lives.

Why is it so *hard* to keep our vehicles clean of clutter? And if you can't keep your car clean, how can you expect to keep up in other areas of your life?

The only way to keep up with clutter is to attack it head-on.

No One Likes Cleaning

No one enjoys cleaning up. It's not a fun job. In fact, it can be downright irritating.

If you don't do it right, it can be a fun little exercise in lowering your self-esteem. A few weeks of chaos and you suddenly find yourself one day staring blankly at your personal leaning tower of Pisa. The dishes are about to reach the heavens. Clutter covers every surface. The self-flagellation begins. Naturally, you start blaming yourself for making the mess in the first place. Or for leaving the mess for later.

Cleaning up after yourself and your family is an important task. Research has shown that a clean workspace is far more conducive to productivity than a messy one. Cleanliness creates a safe space for organization, creativity, and visibility. How could you expect to have a formative, rewarding life with a desk full of things half-done?

In your home, a clean space is safer and calming. You won't trip over items, and you can relax without worrying about the mess. And again, you simply won't be as prone to losing things.

Okay, so here are the sweat-inducing questions: How is your house? Your desk? Your closet?

If you answered, "a mess" to all of the above, chances are that mess didn't happen overnight. So, you can't expect to get it all back to clean in an instant.

Eat the Elephant, Bite-by-Bite

Chances are you have at *least* one huge cleaning job to take care of in your house. Maybe it is the garage. Or a spare bedroom. Or even your closet.

These large jobs can be overwhelming and take many hours to complete. Just *thinking* about their devastating size can be enough to cause you to continue to put them off. A nap is a common response.

Unless you have a full day or weekend to dedicate to these large jobs, something like organizing a coup-d'état of your mess can feel demoralizing. No wonder you keep putting it all off!

One stealthy time-saving technique that I use to tackle these big cleanup jobs is to *eat the elephant, bite-by-bite*. No, please, not literally. Instead of contributing to the impending extinction of elephants, try using the metaphor for good. Designate *fifteen minutes* each morning to take a bite out of the big mess.

It can be disheartening to try and clean up a whole room (or house). But, when you know you only have to do it for fifteen minutes, what was previously ghastly task becomes exceedingly manageable.

Fifteen minutes each day...and with a week you will see a significant dent in even the biggest jobs. How about that for time ninja moves?

While this can be a powerful technique to clean up those large jobs, how do you prevent these elephant jobs from occurring in the first place?

Teeny Messes Make Earth-Shattering Messes

Cleaning left undone piles up and multiplies. Teeny messes are the viruses of the cleaning world.

Some messes will literally make more messes...like unwashed dishes. Ever tried scrubbing days-old grease? Yikes.

What an alert time ninja does is address these messes as *soon* as they occur, not days later when you're wondering if you're going to have to use a plastic fork again tonight (what are you, a broke college student?). You will save so much time by cleaning up preemptively. Trust me.

Dishes in the sink is a great example of messes creating bigger messes. It may take only a few seconds to address immediately, but, leave it until the next day, and you have a much worse cleaning job.

Know Your ABCs

Like many of the productivity methods we have discussed, cleaning needs to be a regular habit, not an event that only happens when things pile up.

ABC = Always Be Cleaning

When? Where? How?

↝ When: During the start of your day, end of your day, and five minutes every now and then

109

❧ Where: Here and there (a.k.a. *wherever* you see a slight mess)

❧ How: By taking the few extra steps to put things away. When in doubt, throw it out

If you practice the art of always cleaning up after yourself when finishing an activity—whether it is putting away tools after a chore, cleaning up the kitchen after a meal, or even folding the laundry after it is done—then you will *never* have a mess to clean up later.

It's an easy habit, but one that most people do not practice.

"Always Be Cleaning" takes a few minutes, but you will regret it if you put it off until later.

Always Be Cleaning

Keeping clean is easier than cleaning up later.

Back to the car example! (Which, by the way, is a question most people hate being asked.)

If you are guilty of cluttering up your car, chances are you're cluttered in other areas of your life.

There is an interesting exception to the dirty car rule—when you have a new car. It's shiny and oh-so-clean, straight out of the sweet-smelling car shop. It's the honeymoon period, and so you go out of your way to keep your beloved *spotless*. It may remain this way for a few months or even a few years. Eventually, the luster wears off and your darling car becomes another victim to clutter.

Our beloved time management ninja principle is right there in that example: *keeping something clean is easier than cleaning it up later.*

This holds true for *all* areas of your life. If you clean your desk for five minutes each day, it *will* stay clean. No way around it. This is infinitely better than one day realizing that your desk is so covered in stuff that you need a dumpster, a bulldozer, and possibly a band of trained monkeys to clean it up. Think of this as taking a daily shower. You do not want to spend a whole week without cleaning up.

Same goes with your closet. If you make a rule that you must not dramatically throw clothes onto your closet floor, then you will find that it only takes a few seconds to hang something up after you try outfits on. No more of that dreaded "closet chair." You know, the chair with over thirty-six discarded outfits on it and a peculiar human-shaped shadow in the middle of the night. Wow, that thing is terrifying.

Trouble getting started? I recommend you set a timer for a few minutes and clean up each day. Put your favorite song as the alert tone so you have something to look forward to!

Consistently keep your area clean and tidy! It is *so* much easier than you think to become a true time management ninja. Let the training begin!

Always Be Cleaning and you will find that keeping your work area clean is much more comfortable and

productive than you thought.

Ninja Wisdom

- ✗ Always Be Cleaning (ABC) means addressing teeny fifteen-minute messes before they become ninety-minute monsters.

- ✗ Bite those elephant-sized cleaning jobs fifteen minutes at a time, every day of the year.

Ninja Training

Becoming a productivity ninja means finding that cleaning up becomes natural daily habit. Wisely fighting off your enemy little by little means you will have less mess to address in your life.

Reflect on these lessons by asking yourself the following:

- ✗ How can you work ABC into your daily routine?

- ✗ How can you practice ABC at the beginning and of the day?

- ✗ What elephants do you need to address in your cleaning and organization?

- ✗ Can you schedule fifteen minutes a day to eat that elephant?

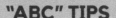

"ABC" TIPS

Here are some tips to Always Be Cleaning:

✖ **Put Things in Their Place:** An essential habit of keeping your space organized is to have a "designated home" for each item. Not only will it be easier to put things away, but you will know right where they are when you need an item again. Tip 9 is ESSENTIAL here!

✖ **Throw Things Out:** Disposing of clutter needs to be a *regular* habit in your cleanup process. You just *cannot* keep everything that comes your way! Most of the items you are keeping have no further use, plain and simple. Don't be a packrat when it comes to papers, trinkets, and more. *When in doubt, throw it out.* A ninja travels light.

✖ **Don't Leave a Mess for Later:** It can be tempting to tell yourself that you will just "put things away later or tomorrow." Resist that alluring excuse. The only perfect moment for cleaning up is <u>now</u>. *Always* clean up immediately after finishing a project. Otherwise, you are compounding the amount of future cleaning you will have to do.

✖ **Have a Chore List:** A schedule for chores can help keep you in regular cleanup mode. Streamline this process by setting up routine maintenance tasks for specific days of the week. Maybe Monday is your clean-off-your-desk day. Tuesday is your document-scanning day. Wednesday is your dusting-your-taxidermy-collection day. And so on.

✖ **Eat Those Elephants:** Big cleanup tasks are easily attacked a little bit at a time. Kind of like cutting up large chunks of food so that they can cook faster. Spend fifteen minutes catching up on that big task and soon you will have whittled it down to a manageable task. Of course, after cleaning becomes a habit, you should have less "elephant" tasks.

✖ **Designate Clean Zones:** Clean Zones are areas that you pledge to *always* keep clean. Designate trouble spots (like desktops, file cabinets, or any other horizontal surface where clutter tends to pile up) as clean zones and never allow pandemonium to ensue in these areas.

✖ **Have Cleanup Time Every Day:** Kindergarten isn't over. Cleanup time is *definitely* still a thing. Schedule fifteen minutes of cleanup time each day. Perhaps, first thing when you come home. Or, if you are *really* disciplined, before heading out. Put it right on your calendar so that you allocate time for it.

TIP 11

ONE EXTRA TASK
A DAY KEEPS
PROCRASTINATION AWAY

*Do one extra task each day that you
have been avoiding.*

How often you do get to the end of your day and realize that you didn't get around to many of the tasks you had intended? How about *none* of them? Those projects end up rolling over to the next day or even put off until some future date. Think February 30 (a.k.a. never). Unfortunately, rollover is only good for your cellphone plan.

According to recent data, the average American has *fourteen* undone tasks that are floating on their to-do list.

Your to-do list should be a running list that is always tracking your tasks! Not a list of future regrets.

If you aren't careful, specific tasks *will* hide themselves in your list. They're there, but can you see them? Before you know it, your undone task list is growing and growing until this backlog starts to bog your mind down. Or, perhaps, some of the formerly non-urgent tasks are now becoming enormous issues because they have been sitting for so long. Both are stealthy of anxiety-inducers.

You must be sneakier than these elusive tasks. Attack them with lightning-fast ferocity.

What tasks have been lurking on your to-do list for an extended time?

Do One Thing You Have Been Putting Off

If you are following Tip 3, then you have ONE master list for your to-dos.

Yet, you probably have tasks that linger on your revered list. I call these *lurkers*. Lurkers freeload on your to-do list for months. In some cases, *years*!

While they may not be your highest priority, they are pesky, stressful burdens. How could you not be tense? They take up your mind and thoughts since you are continually remembering that you have been putting them off and off.

Here's a spooky thought—*you may worry that you will never catch up on these floating tasks.*

One of the best ways to keep up with these procrastinated tasks is to pick off one task each day that you would've otherwise left undone on your list. This project is *not* meant to take over your day. After all, you should be putting the majority of your effort toward your most important tasks. But...

If you attack just one lurking task each day, then keeping up with your to-do list will become a breeze. Regret-less days, here we come!

Whittle Down that List

Sharply examine your to-do list and see how many long-lasting to-dos you have.

You may find these creatures of comfort hanging out in the seedy underbelly of your list. They are indolent bottom-feeders. Regularly being carried over from one day to the next. They are there, sucking the blood out of your otherwise unblemished to-do list.

Or they could be staring at you with insolence, parading on your "maybe someday" list. Knowing you won't have the courage to pry them off, one by one.

Here are some types of tasks that tend to linger on to-do lists:

+ Renew your license with the DMV

+ Make that doctor or dentist appointment

+ Look for a new job

+ Clean up the garage or another intimidating area of your house

+ Get maintenance done on your car

+ Change the air filters in your home

+ Pay the bills

+ Write your will

+ Send a letter to someone you have been meaning to connect with

+ Organize your closet

+ Tidy up the inside of your car

+ Sell miscellaneous items that you no longer need

+ Donate space-taking items to a local charity

- ✦ Collect and review your photos (or maybe digitize old prints)

- ✦ Frame a picture or photograph that you bought but never hung up

- ✦ Book a vacation

All of these tasks are examples of items that many people have trouble getting around to doing. *Yet, most of them would only take a few minutes to complete.*

Why are you putting them off?

- ✦ You don't know what the first step is and are not willing to put in the effort to learn how to start.

- ✦ You don't know how long they're going to take so avoid them.

- ✦ You are too busy and always find more pressing things to do.

None of these are valid reasons, only excuses. You can fit those neglected tasks into your day. Quite frankly, it's easier than *ever* to look up how to do specific tasks. And even you just don't *want* to do them, they aren't just going to go away like some miscellaneous tasks. No, paying your bills *will* haunt you.

Let's see what happens if you *do* end up spending fifteen minutes completing one of those dog-eared tasks a day.

- ✦ In a *week*, that's *seven* things that you have caught up on.

✦ *Thirty* completed to-dos in a *month* that would have otherwise been left untouched.

✦ That's a huge *365* procrastinated tasks that would be overcome in a year!

You will surprise yourself what this rule and a little discipline can accomplish.

Ninja Wisdom

✘ Designate one task each day that you have been avoiding or were probably going to push off.

✘ Do that *one* extra task today and give it utmost priority.

✘ Doing it earlier in your day will motivate you *and* prevent a more significant disruption of your activities.

✘ Follow this powerful nugget of wisdom, young ninja, and you will finally trim your task backlog, one task at a time. This means you can address tasks that may not be urgent now but will become so if ignored.

Ninja Training

Now *you* can put these ninja skills to the test. Only through unforgiving scrutiny can we become masters of time. What tasks have been hanging out on your list for weeks or months, guzzling up your motivation? (Okay, maybe that's an exaggeration, but those suckers can *really* drain you.)

✘ Review your to-do list and identify some tasks that you will begin to address.

✘ Name *one* extra task that you will do today that otherwise would have been put off.

✘ Using Tip 4, make an appointment for this additional task and schedule time to complete it on your calendar. Do this even if it only requires a few minutes of attention.

THE SLIPPERY SLOPE OF "SOMEDAY" LISTS

Most people keep an area on their master to-do list for "someday" tasks. In fact, many task-tracking apps anticipate this desire and have this functionality built in.

Sure, a someday list is an excellent place for keeping tasks that you may not *need* doing right now but that you *may* want to do eventually.

However, someday lists can become slippery slopes when it comes to tasks that *do* need to be completed. Once they are on your someday list, they are out of sight and (too often) out of mind.

Someday lists are where tasks go to hide and be procrastinated. These tasks will haunt you indefinitely if you let them. I've known people who have had tasks on their someday lists for *years*. A friend of mine was telling me that he had been meaning to update his family will due to the birth of his daughter, but had been putting this task off for so long that his daughter *is now six years old*!

"Doing one task that you weren't going to do today" is a powerful method to conquer your "someday" tasks (ones that, once done, can add meaning and order to your life) before they become "never" tasks.

TIP 12

NEVER CONFUSE BUSY

WITH PRODUCTIVE

Busy doesn't get important work done.

Have you ever had a hectic day where you literally do not stop moving from dawn to dusk? You find yourself running, running, running, without the time to stop and eat or even take a break.

Finally, you plop down on the couch, practically heaving, feeling like you ran all day long but accomplished very little.

That unnerving sensation is not wrong. In fact, you look back at your to-do list and find that, while you were oh-so busy, you didn't get to your most important tasks.

How is that even possible after you were working so hard?

Productivity Gets the Work Done

This is a tough one. Often, we *crave* being busy. It seems like the harder you work, the more results you should produce.

However, it only *seems* that way. This mode of thinking confuses being *busy* with being *productive*.

Picture that same stifling, busy day, but with a twist. Rather than engaging immediately with the countless tasks that come your way, you decide to work on the most pressing priorities from your list instead. Looking over your to-do list at the end of the day becomes *so* much more fulfilling.

It's not about doing more. It's about doing more of what's important. Actually, you could even argue that is it about doing less of the things that don't matter.

This is particularly true in your personal life. You only have so much free time, and you should spend it on the people and priorities that matter to you.

Beware of Busyness at Work

The workplace is an ironic example of productivity for most people. If you are learning productivity from your job, you are *probably* being taught bad habits. (By probably, I mean most definitely.)

Many businesses mistakenly reward *busy* rather than *effective*. They reward those who run around and *look* busy versus those who *actually* produce the results. This is a challenge for most companies.

I'm not kidding when I say this is common practice. I have personally seen organizations that actually *reward* busyness. There is, for example, a company that gave an award to an executive who sent the most emails. Another company recognized an employee who was known to always be working 24/7.

Unfortunately, in both of these examples, these two employees were recognized by their peers as highly ineffective. Not only were they busy instead of productive, but they were known in the workplaces for actually making it *harder* for others to do their jobs.

Yet, from a distance busy does look productive. After all, lots of action has to produce lots of results! Right?

Not necessarily.

Here are a few busier but not productive stories from the workplace:

❧ A senior executive who said that he purposefully ran in the office hallways. "After all," he said, "if people see I am in a hurry they know I must be doing something important." (He really said this.)

❧ A manager who was famous for calling meetings for *anything*. Even if he just needed to ask someone a question, he would call a meeting to discuss what could have been a simple email or phone call.

Busyness does not equal results in the workplace. Companies that reward this counterproductive behavior are not destined for success.

Do Less and Get More Done

So, you want to become productive and NOT busy? Becoming an effective ninja means deliberately addressing your actions and time. Rather than rushing maniacally through your day, take your time and focus on what's most important.

You have probably seen successful people who seem to glide effortlessly through their day while everyone else is skittishly running around. Their secret? They know the difference between busy and productive, and they don't waste time on activities that don't produce value.

These individuals may actually "do less" than their peers yet have a more significant impact on results.

So, next time you find yourself blindly scrambling through your day, *stop and refocus*. Examine if what you are doing is productive or if it is just busy work.

You can get more done when you do less. Less of the trivial, and more of what's important. Here are a few tips to help you stay productive rather than busy:

- ↳ **Prioritize your tasks:** As mentioned before, very few people prioritize their to-do lists. In fact, even very few to-do apps provide the functionality necessary for putting your list in priority order quickly. Work your list from most important to least.

- ↳ **Schedule your day:** Making appointments with your personal work (Tip 4) and planning your day (Tip 6) and will ensure that you maximize your schedule each day.

- ↳ **Concentrate on finishing tasks:** A few completed important tasks will always outperform lots of tasks started but not finished.

- ↳ **Live in the present:** Give your full attention to the task at hand. Focus leads to results.

Ninja Wisdom

✖ Busyness doesn't equate to getting important things done.

✖ You can do less and still accomplish more when you focus on your priorities.

✖ Haste doesn't produce results. Focus on priorities delivers value.

Ninja Training

Reflect on your recent workdays.

1. Do you find yourself continually rushing?

2. Are you able to concentrate on priorities? Or are you so busy that you work on whatever is in front of you at any given moment?

3. What important tasks do you have pending that you feel you should give more importance to?

4. What do you need to eliminate from your busy day to allow you to be more effective?

BEWARE OF BUSY MEETINGS

Meetings in the workplace deserve a special word of caution. They get a bad rap for all the right reasons. Meetings are one of the biggest time-wasters at many companies.

Surveys have measured that managers spent upwards of thirty percent of their time in meetings. That number rises to over *fifty* percent for executives.

We have all heard the phrase "death by meeting." Unfortunately, it's a sentiment shared by far too many company workers. Managers don't take the hint. When faced with an issue, the kneejerk reaction of many company leaders is to call a meeting. Before long, the team is spending more time in meetings than doing their work.

Many of these managers mean well, but their last-ditch efforts are ultimately disappointing acts of self-sabotage. They entangle their employees in endless meetings rather than letting them solve the problems in the first place, hands-on. Even worse, the majority of meetings are poorly planned and executed which leads to even *more* wasted time. They lack agendas, have too many attendees, and don't result in any tangible after-action.

Now, not *all* meetings are bad. They can be a great way to get a team on the same page or to brainstorm solutions. However, meeting for meeting's sake is not productive.

Beware the workplace that spends more time in meetings than actually doing the work. These companies are guilty of confusing busy for productive. The last thing we want as time management ninjas is anything remotely like busy work.

YOU CAN'T FINISH IF YOU

DON'T START

*Goals cannot be accomplished if they
are never begun.*

I was talking to a friend recently about our lives, and he expressed that he wasn't sure he "had enough time left" to complete some of his big goals. He was close to retirement, and it was hitting him that he had put off many of his big ambitions. In many cases, his personal goals had always taken a backseat to his job.

One of these goals was to teach a class on leadership to pass along much of what he had learned in his career.

I asked him how long he had been contemplating instructing this class. He thought for a few moments, and finally said, "Wow, almost ten years." I could hear a break in his voice near the end.

"And why haven't you ever done it?"

"Well, I guess I never started it," was his soft reply. "I always thought I would get to it *someday.*"

Someday Isn't on the Calendar

What have you been telling yourself that you would do someday? Likely, you'll think about this for a few moments like my friend did.

Once you do think of something (which is highly likely), I need you to know something very important:

Dreams never get done *someday.*

My calendar runs from Monday to Sunday, but there isn't a "Someday" on it.

" 'Someday' isn't a real day like Monday or Tuesday;
it's just another word for 'never.' "
—*Robert Herjavec*, The Will To Win: Leading,
Competing, Succeeding

And that's the problem. If you are planning on achieving your dreams on "Someday," that day is *never* going to arrive.

You have to start. You can't afford to wait. You have to do it with the only day you have, which is *today*.

Now, you may sarcastically say that "Today" isn't on the calendar either. Haha, very funny. Well, I disagree on *all* fronts. It is on the calendar every day. Every time you wake up, it's today. It is the one day that you can control and can act upon.

You need to start today.

Start Small but Start Today

What prevents many people from starting on their goals is that they are intimidated. They don't know where or how to begin. Maybe they may not even understand what is required.

That is okay. What matters is that you *start*, no matter how small that start seems.

Even the smallest step each day is progress and moves you forward toward your goal. No pressure. No prejudices. Don't preemptively fail yourself.

135

Want to write a book? Jot down some notes or an outline.

Want to get in shape? Hit the gym or even go for a walk.

Want to learn a new skill? Research the topic to get an overview. Or sign up for a class.

Want to get started on a new career? Look for a job.

Just one step forward today will make all the difference tomorrow. Progress compounds, so, the more you put in what you do today, the greater the success you will have in the future.

You don't have to climb a mountain today to accomplish your goal. Yet, each step forward builds measurable progress toward success.

The Danger of Talking about Your Goals

As a side note, there are some who believe that you shouldn't ever talk about your goals with others. They claim that by talking about the things you want to do you actually prevent action. I disagree. I think your aspirations should always be at the forefront of your mind. I also believe that you should tell *others* about your specific plans.

Speaking about your dreams makes them real and holds you accountable.

However, recent studies have shown that there is considerable risk in *only* talking about your goals. If you are all talk and no action, you can actually perpetuate the deferment of your dreams.

The trap many people fall into is that they confuse *talking* about their goals with starting them. *Talk is good, but it must be followed up with action.*

When you discuss your goals with friends or family, make sure you are talking about the steps you are taking now and the ones you will take in the future.

Goals without a Deadline Are Just Dreams

"A goal is a dream with a deadline."
—Napoleon Hill

This is the harsh reality: you will fail at every goal you never undertake.

Dreams are goals that you just talk about but never take action toward. *To make your dreams happen, you have to begin.*

Want to know how you can screw up your goals? Don't start working on them.

It's *not* about writing them down. (A great tactic!)

It's *not* about talking about them. (A great way to be held accountable!)

You have to *start* them.

Most people will never actually *start* their goals.

A good friend of mine talked to me years ago about writing a book. (It's an *intense* endeavor, I'm telling you.) But every time I would see him and ask about it, he would sheepishly say that he was just far too busy with work or family to get around to it. Yet, he kept telling me that he wanted more than anything to publish a series of books.

Many years later we crossed paths again and the same old question came up. No, he still had not begun writing his books. Yet, he *was* still talking about this goal. He suddenly decided enough was enough. He would start writing at last, even if it would be just some notes here and there.

Before he knew it, he had several notebooks filled with story ideas for his books. That was nutritive substance, he told me. Sitting down to write, it all started to flow. Now? He has not only written his trilogy, he is just about to publish his fourth book!

Whatever it is...you have to *take that first step*. Otherwise, you literally have no chance of ever accomplishing your goal.

You won't reach any goal that you never begin.

What have you always wanted to do?

You don't want to look back many years hence and say, "If only I had started. If only I had taken that first small step."

Some people go their entire lives without ever *attempting* to follow through on their big goals.

138

They are comfortably satisfied with the status quo. Or they are just drifting, eyes blanking on black mirror screens. It's scary when you find that you may be in that situation.

They sure like to *talk* about what they want to do someday. But they never get around to *doing* it. That's not the time ninja way.

So, whatever your big goals are...make sure you start them. Your world of inner peace and self-fulfillment is at stake.

Ninja Wisdom

✗ You can't accomplish the goals that you never start.

✗ "Someday" *never* comes along.

✗ Only ever talking about goals does not move them forward.

✗ Your goals need deadlines, or else they remain just dreams.

✗ A small step forward each day is excellent progress.

Ninja Training

We all have things that we dream of. They do not deserve to be put off and off.

✗ What is on your bucket list? Your *life* list? (I like that term better.) Better put, *what do you want to accomplish in your before you die*? It should be an easy question and immediately in your mind. We all have things that we want to "do someday."

✗ Now, make a list of twenty things that you want to do in your lifetime.

140

START ON YOUR BUCKET LIST

In our dystopia-obsessed, hyper-aware, globalized world, the concept of the "bucket list" has become very popular. It's kind of morbid and a little fascinating. Derived from the English idiom for death ("kick the bucket"), it lists the things people want to start, but have never gotten around to doing.

Here are some common bucket list items:

✘ Travel the world

✘ Run a marathon

✘ Write a book

✘ Learn to play an instrument

✘ Skydive

✘ Own a pet

✘ Get a tattoo

✘ Learn another language

✘ Drive across the country

✘ See your favorite band or musician in concert

✘ Go camping

✘ Climb a mountain

✘ Go scuba diving

✘ Swim in the ocean

Each of these is absolutely achievable! You just need to *start*.

TIP 14

REALIZE YOU ARE

STRONGER THAN

YOU THINK

*"Whether you think you can,
or you think you can't—you're right."*
—Henry Ford

I am here, writing on my laptop during an ungodly hour, to tell you that you are more capable than you think.

You *can* do more than you believe.

You *can* reach levels that you don't dream are possible.

And that is part of the issue. *You don't believe that you can do it.* When it comes to reaching new levels of performance, it's your own beliefs that limit you. And, well...

Most people limit themselves more than the world does.

You might be asking yourself what this tip has to do with time management. One word: goals. If time management is your goal, realize you can not only get more time back, but become a full-fledged time management ninja. You are capable.

Self-Imposed Limits

We have a family pet—a sweet, lovable dog. When she was a puppy, we trained her not to go into certain rooms of our house. We did this by using a puppy-sized door gate across the room entrances.

The interesting thing is that, even though she is an adult now, our dog will *still* not go into those rooms. The door gates are no longer there, but she will stand in the doorway as if they were.

She is the only one limiting her travel. In her mind, she still sees the limits.

This may seem like just a cute pet story, but it is also an example of how beliefs create perceived limits.

> *Unconsciously, you probably have restrictions in your mind that you have set on your life.*

What I have observed is that most people impose their *own limits.* They limit their output based on self-framed constraints of their capabilities and strengths. Sometimes these boundaries are based on past experiences. Sometimes they are based on preconceived capacities. Sometimes these limits are based on literally *nothing.*

I can't do that. (*Why?*)

That is too much for me. (*How do you know?*)

I can't put in that much effort. (*What would happen if you did?*)

I am not smart enough to solve that. (*Can you be sure if you haven't tried?*)

So, how do we break through these limits? How do we get *stronger?*

What Is Strength?

Strength is not always about pure physical strength. (Rarely so, in our modern world.)

Rather, it is about willpower. Discipline. Drive. It is about the capacity to get things done.

I know some people who are *intellectually* strong, but get very little done in their jobs. On the other hand, I know others who find work extremely challenging yet are able to move *mountains* with their sheer drive and hard work.

They possess *inner strength*.

More interestingly, is that these productive hard workers often don't even notice the sheer load they carry! Bystanders are not only amazed, but often ask, "How do you do it?"

The answer usually comes back, "I just work harder than the others."

So, why are some people able to do more? What gives them added drive? What gives them that extra strength?

Could it be they have simply given themselves permission to do more?

Pushing It...

Ironically, even though we are talking about inner strength, one of the best places to see self-imposed limitations is at the gym. Yes, that nexus of outer strength. I see people go through the motions of working out—the whole earbuds blasting, sweat dripping on the rubber mat—but are nowhere *near* their strength limits. They wave a bunch of lightweight dumbbells in the air, and then wonder why they are not seeing results. Many of them could probably lift twice the amount of weight they are using.

Pushing it is what it takes to increase your limits. Bodybuilders discovered this long ago. But the same principle is true when it comes to inner strength. Discipline and drive.

If you want to be stronger and accomplish more, you have to push your boundaries. Real life is a gym. What lightweight dumbbells are you carrying?

_____

Want to test your limits? Push yourself. Test your self-perceived constraints to see how accurate they are. Make sure your goals are slightly beyond what you think can be achieved.

_____

You Are More Capable than You Think

Maybe you haven't even attempted to address you goals because you lack the belief that you can accomplish them. From a logical standpoint, this is understandable—you probably haven't reached your goal before.

For example, my friend had on her bucket list to run a marathon. However, she had never run a 5K race before. In fact, she wasn't a runner at all. A marathon may have been her goal, but she had fully convinced herself that she simply did not have the physical stamina.

Maybe she didn't at the moment, but it was her *mind*, not her *body* that was holding her back.

A change in perspective was direly necessary. She started running—short distances at first. Within a few months, she ran her first 5K race. Okay, maybe she *could* run, she thought. No kidding! Not only that, she discovered that she also enjoyed the physical and mental release running gave her.

She had changed her personal limits from, "I can't run," to "I can run a 5K."

My friend continued training, and over the next year she pushed her internal belief to "I can run a half marathon."

She was in the best shape of her life and had totally changed her subjective beliefs. More importantly, she was much stronger than she thought initially.

You have to push your limits to exceed them.

Comfortable Being Uncomfortable

You are more than able to surpass your limitations. Yet, setting new limits for yourself isn't easy. It requires the supernova trifecta. The ultimate ninja weapon arsenal.

You will need: *hard work, discipline, and time.*

To reach new levels of performance, you have to be willing to leave your comfort zone. In fact, you need to get comfortable with being uncomfortable. You have to get ready to do something you've never done before. Get ready to unlock new potential, young ninja.

Individuals that are bold and adventurous enough to exceed their previous limits are the ones that are successful in improving themselves.

Ninja Wisdom

✖ Your internal beliefs set the limits for your performance.

✖ Only by exceeding your limits can you set new, rewarding ones.

✖ Get comfortable with leaving your comfort zone.

Ninja Training

Use these questions to think about those internal beliefs that are limiting your performance:

✖ What things do you say "I could never do that" to?

✖ What areas in your life have limits that you need to test?

✖ Are you too comfortable with the status quo? Do you feel unsatisfied as a result?

✖ What would you need to do to exceed your current limits?

✖ Think specific. What concrete steps could you take right now to surpass those pesky self-limitations for good?

GETTING UNCOMFORTABLE

One of the best ways to stretch your limits is to leave your comfort zone.

When you are comfortable, you are doing what you have always done. By doing so, you're probably getting the results you have always gotten. It's easy because it's familiar. How could expect to feel satisfied this way?

To test your limits and expand them *you must pursue new experiences*. You need to get uncomfortable in order to discover the new levels of your comfort zone.

Sometimes it is as easy as shaking up your routine. Other times, you will need to push yourself far beyond what you think you are capable of today. Try it out! See what happens.

Here are a few examples of things (ranging from super simple jolts to major upheavals in behavior) that you can do to "get uncomfortable" and expand your limits:

✖ Take a different route to work and see the sights. There are many roads to the same destination.

✖ Try new foods other than what you normally eat.

✖ Change your workout routine to surprise your muscles.

✖ Explore a new physical activity or hobby.

✖ Try saving more money than you thought you could this week. A little frugality may surprise you.

✖ Read a book of a genre or viewpoint that you don't normally read.

✖ Ask for help on something that you have been struggling to accomplish on your own.

✖ Adjust your life goals beyond where you have them currently.

What have you done lately to feel uncomfortable?

KNOW YOU ARE WHAT

YOU DO TODAY

(AND EVERY DAY)

Your habits define who you are.

What did you do today? Perhaps a friend you quickly grabbed a burger with after work asked you that. Maybe you were catching up with your spouse and asked them that when you were winding down from the day.

Chances are, the answer is the same as what you would've given yesterday. And almost every *other* day. We are creatures of habit. And if you stop to think about it, you really *do* most of the same things every day.

You have the same morning routine. You usually eat and drink the same thing for breakfast and during the day.

Okay, maybe not *every* meal, but the majority of them. (And when you go to a restaurant, you order the same thing probably 80 percent of the time.)

Beyond your food habits, you carry the same items, and you do many of the same actions every day. You go through the same motions, the same activities, and the same schedule.

But just what *are* those activities? And more importantly, are they leading you in the right direction or down a path of ruin? Whatever those habits do, they do it *every single day*.

Think about it, in which direction are your habits moving you?

What Do You Want to Do Today?

Strangely, when you hear people talk about their habits, they are *actually* referring to things that they want to begin

154

incorporating into their future. Sound familiar? That's the *whole* premise behind New Year's resolutions.

Those habits people talk about are usually *aspirational* habits, not *everyday* habits. But it's the things that you do *today*, what you did *yesterday*, and what you do *every single day* that define who you are.

> *People aspire to be something today, yet they aren't doing it today.*

Talking about habits may make you uneasy. Queasy. You may be frustrated or anxious about the practices you aren't doing today. While all *that's* going on, you can't help but get sheepishly fazed about the things that you *are* doing today that you just shouldn't be. The bad habits.

> *These activities are your daily habits. And they are either making you better or worse each day.*

Good vs. Bad Habits

We *all* have habits. Some are good, some are bad, and most of us have a few evil ones.

The good ones are the ones that move you closer to the ideal *you* that you've always wanted to be. They help you live the life you desire. These good habits may be eating right, working out, studying, consistently investing in your relationships, and more. (Once you become a time management ninja you'll hopefully have more than your fair share of these.)

The bad habits are the ones that take you down a negative path. They drag you backwards and down—the exact *opposite* of the direction you want to go in. If you have been trying unsuccessfully to get physically fit, then one of your bad habits might be not getting enough rest. Your exhaustion will not only prevent your body from operating at peak performance, but will probably keep you from going to the gym altogether. The same can be said of eating junk food or drinking too much. These activities are taking you further *away* from your goal.

You have to ask, "Are your habits making you better or worse each day?"

You are what you do every single day.

But, how do you stay on top of your good habits? And keep the bad ones at bay?

Have a Daily Routine

You are what you do every single day. You are only a writer if you write every day. You are only a basketball player if you hit the court day in and day out. It's that simple. As a time management ninja on a mission to take back control of your life, it is *imperative* for you to do the work to get the results.

You want to get in shape, but you don't work out.

You want to start a new career, but you don't apply to new jobs or put in the time to learn new skills.

You want to learn a new language, but you don't even know how to say "hello" in that language.

One of the best ways to stay true to the habits you want is to have a daily routine. We are creatures of habit, and we like doing the same things with regularity. Establishing a daily routine can ensure that you *stick* with your good practices and avoid the ones that take you off track.

Having a daily routine lets you get your habits done with less effort. If you *always* workout before you start your day, it becomes routine. If you *always* clean up your workspace before you leave work each day, it becomes a habit. If you *always* jump up and down three times before you eat ten apples at noon, *it becomes a habit.*

When you define your routine, you are defining who you are going to be each day.

Ninja Wisdom

✘ Good habits build you up, while evil habits are self-destructive.

✘ Today is the one day you can affect with any degree of certainty.

✘ A routine ensures that you consistently practice your habits.

✘ You are fully defined by your daily habits.

Ninja Training

Our daily patterns are so self-ingrained that we often aren't fully aware of them until a book like this points them out. What are your daily habits?

✘ Delineate your daily routine.

✘ What good habits do you already have that you want to make sure you do every day? What new good habits do you want to start replacing bad ones with?

✘ Which evil ones do you urgently need to completely eliminate?

✘ How will you track your habits to ensure liability?

SIXTY-SIX DAYS TO MAKE (OR BREAK) A HABIT

A recent study showed that forming a habit takes (on average) about sixty-six days. That is a little over two months before an activity becomes comfortably part of your routine. Interestingly, it takes about the same amount of time to break a bad habit and prevent it from coming back.

Can you go the distance to form a new habit? Time to use these sixty-six days for good, young ninja.

Here are some tips:

✗ **Have an accountability partner:** Have a friend or loved one fiercely hold you to your new habit. Make a point to check in *regularly* with them with your progress. Maybe you can eventually hold *each other* accountable! This is so much fun! Woo!

✗ **Use a habit tracker:** You can even use paper (fancy bullet journal style or old-school black pen), but your smartphone can be a formidable ninja weapon, too. Edgy apps that can easily track your rituals for you *and* annoy you until you get the job done! I use Habit List on my iPhone, but you can use anything that will pester you repeatedly!

✗ **Track habit breaking, too:** Can you go sixty-six days without indulging in that pesky behavior you are trying to break? (Like *not* scarfing down cake at three a.m. every Tuesday?) After a month, you will find that you have moved on to, well, more positive actions than binge-eating Twinkies while chugging Mountain Dew.

IS YOUR LIFE ON REPEAT?

When you sit down and think about it, most of us live the same life every single day.

Get up. Get ready. Go to work or school. Come home. Relax. Go to sleep. Start over the next day.

Living our lives on repeat. Living our lives on repeat. Living our lives on repeat. You notice when you read the same sentence over and over, but do you notice when you're living the same day over and over? Will you become a self-aware character in *Groundhog Day*? Unless we become time ninjas and follow our self-mission piously, we are condemned to forever circle around the same activities. Activities that don't fulfill us. Activities, rather, that drain our spirits.

You would *think* we would get it right. Well, actually, we do. You have probably gotten pretty good at repeating your day. So good, in fact, that you don't even *notice* it happening.

Is this day worth repeating?

If not, you have to change your routine. And if you're not getting the results you want, you have to change your habits. Your life is far too important to let its days blend together.

USE YOUR TECH FOR

GOOD, NOT EVIL

Technology should be your friend, not your enemy.

Do you own your technology, or does it own *you*?

You might find yourself squirming after reading that. It's okay if you writhe your fingers in angst. After all, you carry your technology with you everywhere. It is ever-present. Right now, I bet its warming up your right thigh. *Or maybe these words are on its screen!* Ninja, you must be warned.

Technology is both wonderful and terrible at the same time. A potent weapon of mass distraction and joy. At the same time.

Acts unthinkable decades past—instantly speaking to someone in Siberia while you're in Hawaii, choosing songs that match your heartbeat—are absolutely feasible now.

Remember what I said in the very beginning? Like it or not, we're constantly cheating on others with our phones. How could we not? Our bewitching iPads, Apple Watches, Pixel and Galaxy phones have *anything* we could possibly desire and decidedly hate available right under our fingertips.

Yes, all these gadgets were made to make our lives *easier*. More enjoyable. That's why it is of *utmost* importance that we not let this power be used for others' conveniences or our own demise.

Make Sure Your Tech Is a Positive Influence

Lock yourself in your room. Gather everything remotely technological and place it on your bed. No one else can be there (they might call a psychiatric hospital). Now that the whole gang's here, I need you to ask your devices one question: *who's really in charge here?*

They might start humming. Buzzing uncontrollably. *You must remain calm.* It is likely they have never been asked that before. But if they *do* light up and come alive when you ask, then you know the answer.

Your technology might be a hindrance rather than a helper in your day-to-day life.

Unfortunately, devices have become so ubiquitous that most people don't even *realize* how much they have taken over. They monopolize so much of your time that it is amazing that anything gets done. Honestly, I say you've done a pretty good job on your life work so far, considering these buzzing beings.

Trust me, I don't mean to sound like a mopey traditionalist, but our present situation really does look pretty dire. You've seen this scene before—people ambling around gawking at tiny screens, little kids watching videos in parks rather than running around, couples on dates with pupils dilating because of their phone lights and not each other.

They're not the only ones. People are spending upwards of *ten hours a day* looking at gadget screens. But *why* are we on our phones for so long if social media actually *reduces* overall happiness?

Unfortunately, it all boils down to biology. Your reward centers absolutely *tingle* whenever you get those incessant notification messages. One dopamine spike after another and suddenly you're addicted. Cell phones manufacturers such as

Apple have even implemented tools like Screen Time to help you track, well, your screen time.

In conclusion, your phone, (tablet, whatever it is this time), shouldn't run your life.

It is a *tool* for when *you* need it, not for when *it* needs *you*.

> Yet, if you let it...your technology will not only run
> your life, but it will also ruin your life.

Stop Having an Affair with Your Phone

Your phone has all the answers to any possible questions. It plays you your favorite music. How did it shuffle to the exact melody you needed? It endearingly corrects your spelling. It saves every picture you both take. It knows how to recognize your voice, fingerprint, face. It knows you. Better than anyone else. So shiny, quiet, with the confidence of someone who knows they've got you. You wish you could will a notification from them into existence.

Buzz...

Wait, is that...No! It can't be!

...Zzz... Zzz!...

Ah! Yes! It just vibrated. A notification. It seemed to call out for your attention. It needs you!

You look at me abjectly and say, "It's innocent, Craig! I swear!"

I've heard it all before.

"I'm not doing anything illicit! Just playing a game of Fruit Ninja! Generating random results from Wikipedia! Reading about the royal wedding!"

Sure. You're also looking at cat GIFs and cute pet videos on YouTube.

Yet, *how much of that is of value to you? Are you just wasting your time away?*

I am not proposing that we call for a Luddite revival. The key is to be a responsible ninja. To use your technology for good rather than evil.

From a health and safety standpoint, phones have forever altered our world. And that is a *good* thing. If you carry a portable charger, you are always a tap away from being able to call for help anywhere and anytime.

Yet, at the same time, that "anywhere" and "anytime" can be a fierce detriment. It means that our gadgets can interrupt us. Always. Whether we're executives who check our Apple Watches thirty-two times during meetings or leaders who never quite figured out how to silence our iPhones, *all* of us are on the brink of having a full-on affair. With our phones, of course.

The average person checks their phone over one hundred and fifty times per day.

Yes, one hundred and fifty times.

Here are some ways to use your phone as a ninja weapon of good:

- **Minimize your use**: Remember that usage tracker on your phone? Once you know which apps are vampiric, be purposeful in the use of your phone. Notice you spend an inordinate amount of time on YouTube? Limiting usage of it is super easy with this tool. Good rule of thumb is to use phone to be productive. Don't pick it up just to pass time.

- **Delete apps**: Installing apps on our phones is *exciting*. There's an app for virtual cow milking? Yet, all those little apps can be tempting. Delete apps that you don't need or that don't bring value to your life. Be a ruthless abolisher.

- **Clean up that home screen**: What is on your home screen? You may have the factory home screen or absentmindedly set it up. Either way you see it *constantly*, so make sure your home screen only contains your productivity apps. Hide those entrainment apps.

- **Turn off all notifications**: You don't need to know the moment you're tagged in a Facebook post, I promise. Social media notifications are pretty useless, anyway. All your aunt does is post pictures of her thirteen-year-old Pomeranian. Its Mickey Mouse headband was only cute the first seven times.

- **Do Not Disturb mode**: You liked not receiving any pings throughout the day? Try this. First, to prevent any sort of weird accident, set Do Not Disturb up so that you only get notifications for calls from family. Once that's done, try putting the "Do Not Disturb" sign on your virtual hotel door for one whole day. You'll love it. Increment the time

and suddenly you've been with your phone on Do Not
Disturb for years like me.

Ninja Wisdom

✖ Make sure your technology makes your life easier.

✖ Always remember that tech is for *your* convenience, not other people's.

✖ Don't let your gadgets run your life.

✖ Turn off the interruptions, beeps, and ringers. There are very few reasons that your phone needs to make noise or vibrate.

✖ Put the phone down when not required.

✖ Prioritize people over your technology.

Ninja Training

Let's take a look and see if you are using your technology for good or evil.

✖ Make a list of all the positive things your device does for you. These should be things that save you time, provide valuable information, or make life easier.

✖ Make a list of all the negative things you do on your phone. Be compassionless. Some of these activities may even be fun, but *do they add value*? Or are they just that—time-wasters?

✖ Make some new rules for your phone. What specific practices can you put in place to ensure that you are using your phone for good rather than evil?

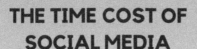

THE TIME COST OF
SOCIAL MEDIA

Data shows that most adults are on social media over an hour a day.

Without debating the merits of this activity, there is a time cost to staying plugged into your social networks.

At least an hour a day, that is seven hours a week. Or 365 hours a year. Likely, it's more.

That is a little over fifteen *days* of social media time. A year. Lost. Forever.

What is your time worth? And what could you accomplish with an extra two weeks each year?

MAKE CHOICES OR

LIFE WILL MAKE THEM

FOR YOU

*"Action speaks louder than words
but not nearly as often."*
—Mark Twain

"Where do you want to go to eat?"

"Oh, I don't know. Where do *you* want to go?"

"I don't know, what do *you* want?"

"I'm fine with whatever you want..."

"I don't care. Anything sounds good..."

"I can't think of any place to go!"

Sound familiar? I'll bet you *lunch* that you have. (I'll decide where.)

How much time do you waste in those bouts of paralyzing indecision?

Simple matters like eating dinner are probably inconsequential if you can't decide on them with confidence. Serious matters, such as where to work, whom to hang out with, whom to marry, how to raise your kids, and what to do in your spare time, can deeply affect your quality of life and that of others.

Whether you make a choice or not...you just did. Choice is the one thing that we all have. And we are constantly making them.

Yet, many people let life make decisions for them, by simply *choosing* not to make a choice.

This could be the most critical topic of the entire book.

I'm not joking. If you cannot make decisions, you won't be able to accomplish many things in your life. What's important, and what's not. What to do, or not to do. What you want to do, and what you'd rather not do.

---

*Life is about choices. Yet, most people choose
not to make them.*

The irony is that the same people often spend an exorbitant amount of time complaining about wanting more control of their lives. Or wanting more success. And wanting more *time*.

Yet, they aren't doing the *one thing* that leads to all of those things. The simple act of choosing.

"Gah! What would I give to get one more week in the year!" Okay, so what if I *did* give you all the time you say you need? Well, here I am. I hereby give you not one, but *three* extra weeks.

Would you really take advantage of that time? Would you even be able to decide what to *do*? Or would you spend more time on your couch, getting thumb cramps?

If you want to get to where *you* want to go, you have to stand up for yourself and your interests. You have to be willing to make choices even when the outcome may not be clear. Even when you may not have all the information that you *think* you need.

Still, you need to make a decision. Your world is counting on you, ninja.

What Are You Choosing to Do?

By choosing to do some things, you are naturally choosing *not* to do others. Better yet, what are you constantly deciding *not* to do?

It might be an eye-opening exercise to make the following two-column list:

What I'm Not Getting Done	What I Am Doing Instead
Instead of going to the gym,	I am choosing to read about Kylie Jenner.
Instead of finishing that important document,	I am choosing to surf Facebook and read my middle school best friend's anti-vaccine posts.
Instead of starting my book of poetry,	I am choosing my phone wallpaper for the eighth time.
Instead of preparing my meal for tomorrow,	I am choosing to drench myself in soda on the couch.

"Instead of doing 'this,' I am choosing to do 'that' can put your time choices in clear perspective. Even when you don't make an explicit decision you are still making the choice to do nothing.

Don't Be Driftwood

When you don't make choices, you are choosing the do-nothing option. (Which *can* be a viable option...it just shouldn't be your default one.)

When you don't make choices, life makes them for you. This can be an easy way to live, but it doesn't result in success or a purposeful time ninja lifestyle.

I call this being driftwood on the river of life.

It's like being on a constant lazy river. While those foolish fish swim against the stream, you're basking in the sunlight of unproductivity. You don't have to sweat the swim. You go with the flow and let life's current direct your course. Yet, you are going where the river takes you, not necessarily where *you* want to go. No one's steering the driftwood.

What eventually happens to driftwood? Over time, the steady stream wears down your edges, colors, and strength. Any jagged rocks or sudden drops? It's game over. You'll get stuck and break apart immediately. Great fun, right?

Being driftwood on the river of life will not give you control over your own destiny.

Decisions Can Be Changed

I hear you ask, "But, what if I make a bad choice?"

Mulling over this question may be what is stopping you. You are so worried about making a "bad" choice that you make no decision at all.

But guess what? If you *don't* choose, the river will make the choice for you.

✦ Don't apply to that new job? It will be taken by someone else.

✦ Don't pursue a new business idea? It will be started by another.

✦ Don't volunteer for an opportunity? It will soon pass, and you will have missed it.

A bad decision is *always* better than no decision at all. There are very few choices in life that cannot be undone later.

There is no need to fear regret. You make the best choices you can at the time, with the best information that you have. *There is never a perfect choice.*

Yet, that is the best part. It's a true leap of faith, one full of excitement, healthy fear, and the unknown. And you just have to trust yourself to make beneficial choices.

Here is a life secret that most people never understand:

With rare exception (such as in cases of health), you can change your mind about nearly every decision you make.

That's right. You can change your mind on even supposedly milestone decisions on things like your career and your relationships. Perhaps you get better information or understanding about the situation. Maybe you suddenly garnered a distaste for it. Either way, there's a U-turn. People aren't perfect. The world is prepared for that.

If you don't like the purchase you made, you can donate it or return it and purchase something different.

If you don't like the job (or career) you have chosen, you have the ability to change it.

If you don't like the relationship you are in, you can leave it.

You can change your mind. You can make another choice. Instead of being driftwood, you are a surfer.

There are very few permanent choices in life.

Make your choices. And relish in your surfer-like ability to make decisions.

Ninja Wisdom

- ✦ Everyone says that they want a choice. Most don't make that decision.

- ✦ Making decisions is a crucial productivity skill. It reduces wasted time and effort.

- ✦ You can change your mind; very few choices are permanent.

Ninja Training

Where do you need to be more decisive in your life? Are you making your own choices, or do you let life make them for you?

Here are a few questions to ask:

- ✦ What decisions are you facing right now?

- ✦ What is keeping you from making a choice about them?

- ✦ How much time have you spent in anxious indecision?

- ✦ What decisions have you made in your life that you want to change?

MAKE TIMELY DECISIONS

Often a quick decision is better than a long drawn out one.

Now, I am not saying to make snap judgements about important moments in your life. Some of those big decisions require long analysis and deep decision-making.

But, *most* of the choices we face every single day are not that life-altering. You are better off making a choice and moving on. You'll save time and gain mental stability. Constant rumination and deliberation can be very frazzling.

Here are five wise tips to help you become a timely-decision ninja:

1. **Make *your* choice**: The ability to make a choice is the greatest gift and a most precious right. Yet, if you don't make choices, then the river will make them for you. So, think about what you want and go with your gut. No driftwood could do that! Only a stealthy ninja surfer could.

2. **Don't wait for a perfect time (or choice)**: As I have said many times, there is no perfect time, there is just *now*. Don't wait for the perfect time, it will literally never come. Similarly, there is *never* a perfect choice. If you wait forever, hoping for a perfect option, you will often find that you missed out on your choice entirely.

3. **Most choices aren't that important**: You might make a bad choice. But the truth is that most decisions just *aren't* that important in the big picture. Don't stress about things that you won't even remember in a month or even year from now.

4. **Flip a coin:** Okay, this tip sounds, well, a bit *flippant*. But most decisions would be better off with a coin toss than no decision at all. Ever spend time driving around trying to decide where to eat? Just flip a coin already. Maybe you'll discover what you really want

5. **Make a choice and enjoy it:** Have you ever made a choice, and then found yourself second-guessing it *before* you have even finished carrying it out? You don't even give yourself the opportunity to experience your decision because you are too busy thinking about those other choices. When you make a choice, *go with it*! And, more importantly, *enjoy it*!

PASSION MAKES YOU

MORE PRODUCTIVE

When you practice your passion, such as a hobby, it makes you more productive in all areas of your life.

So far, we have been talking about saving time by reducing the amount of activities in your life.

Well, you read the title and epigraph of this chapter. What do you think?

"How could you say this? After all you told me! Who even has time for that?!"

You do. Especially if you want to be more motivated in all your endeavors.

Becoming a time management ninja means reducing the amount of *unfulfilling* activities in your life.

A hobby is something you are passionate about. Something that drives and excites you. Having a hobby can actually put more time and energy back in your life.

It doesn't matter if your hobby is weightlifting, taxidermy, reading, surfing, or photography. You just have to be passionate about it.

All Work and No Play

Too many people make the mistake of being *all* business. They think that if they just keep working harder and put in more hours that they will be successful.

Having a hobby is another counter-intuitive rule—a lot like doing less to accomplish more.

You may notice that most successful individuals not only get their work done but also pursue extracurricular activities like golf or travel.

Others watch in an entranced spell from afar, wondering, "How do get their work down *and* have time for a hobby on the side?" These are but frivolous endeavors, we tell ourselves. I'll stick to my nine-to-five and watch Netflix, thank you very much.

But, no! We deserve that life, too!

You are still skeptical.

"What does participating in a hobby have to do with time management and being more productive?"

The answer: *everything*.

Hobbies are something you *enjoy*. They elevate your mood and motivate you. That intoxicating high from doing what you love *will* carry over to your other activities. It's not me making this stuff up, either. Studies have shown that hobbies boost your creative energy and actually lead to quicker mental recovery from work and stress.

That's right.

"Wasting" time on hobbies will help you have a better work life! A ninja needs time off, too. Only then can they become alert productivity masters.

Here are just a few of the things a hobby can increase your overall productivity:

- ↗ **Relax you:** Hobbies reduce stress and allow you to blow off steam.

✦ **Take your mind off work:** That chunk of time you set aside for your passion will let you *finally* stop thinking about work. Ironically, you may find that your brain comes up with solutions to tough problems when you are *not* thinking about them!

✦ **Make you physically fit:** Active hobbies help you keep your body in top physical shape. Your mind was made for a world with constant physical exertion.

✦ **Make you mentally fit:** Many hobbies (intellectual and athletic) provide the opportunity to learn new skills and information. You can develop good habits like patience, problem-solving, and spatial skills.

✦ **Improve your mood:** Hobbies can elevate your mood. After a rough day at work, they can be just what you need to bounce back to a positive mindset.

✦ **Provide an outlet for creativity:** Immersing yourself in the flow of your hobby can give you opportunities for immense creative growth.

Finding Your Hobby

Many people say that they don't know what their hobby should be. Yet, they are quick to say, "I used to do...." So, they *did* have a hobby in the past.

What would you enjoying doing as a kid ninja, outside of school and family life? Which of these activities do you return to when you are feeling overloaded?

If you're still dazed, look at what you read and watch. What types of shows, podcasts, or articles do you enjoy? Chances are you may be "watching" your hobby all the time—you just aren't participating.

When people are too busy at work and decide to come ask me for advice, one of the first things I ask them in return is, "What is your hobby?" To which they respond, "Are you kidding? I don't have *time* for a hobby!"

I tell them, "You don't have time *not* to."

The irony here is that by cutting back on their hobbies they are actually negatively affecting their ability to keep up with their obligations (let alone *exceed* at them). So, it becomes a classic case of self-perpetuation.

Spending more time on yourself will result in more time and productivity at work.

A Hobby Is about Investing in You

When the going gets rough and people start buckling down, they start saying no to themselves first. After all, saying no to others is hard and saying no to yourself is easy.

So, they begin denying themselves the things that keep them happily alive and energized. Leisure activities, sports, spending time with their family? These are the *first* things to go. They're the fancy vases thrown off a sinking ship.

Focusing too much on work and neglecting the

things that renew us will ultimately lead to personal failure. Spend more time on yourself, and you find you are more productive (and happy!) in all areas of your life.

———

Ninja Wisdom

✦ Hobbies offer many positive benefits—from physical fitness to mental stamina.

✦ Spending time on activities that renew your energy levels is *vital* to success.

✦ Having a recreational activity is essential to providing the passion and motivation you need in *all* areas of your life.

Ninja Training

Spend the next minutes closely examining your avocation. If you don't currently have one, it's time to rediscover your school-age passions.

✦ Name two hobbies that you would like to pursue.

✦ How might they make you feel or motivate you?

✦ What obstacles might be in the way of you pursuing your hobby? Are these the same obstacles that were present in the past? How can you address these?

✦ How and when will you pursue your hobbies?

RECLAIM YOUR HOBBY

There are no hard-and-fast rules when it comes to hobbies. They are highly personal by definition. Only thing—your avocation must be something *you* care about and something that *excites* you.

Hobbies truly run the gamut. Everything physical or mental or in between is fair game.

Here are some popular hobbies:

1. Playing sports

2. Reading

3. Playing video games

4. Listening to music

5. Playing an instrument

6. Traveling

7. Collecting (watches, stamps, buttons, artwork)

8. Photography

9. Gardening

10. Home improvement

11. Hiking

12. Working on cars

13. Volunteering

14. Fishing

15. Assisting cultural events

16. Cooking

17. Boating

18. Wine and spirits connoisseurship

19. Writing poetry

20. Keeping a blog

If this list doesn't get your passion's attention, there is a list of several hundred hobbies on Wikipedia. Yay! Using technology for good!

LET IT BE (YOU CAN'T

DO IT ALL)

If you try to do everything, you'll find that you don't accomplish much of anything.

Unfortunately, everyone has a limit as to how much they can take on at once. You just can't do it all. No one can. However, busy people tend to make themselves *busier* by taking on more and more until they can't keep up. They have a problem not taking on new tasks and feel out of control if they are not in charge of everything.

Are you guilty of taking on too much even when you are already overloaded?

Do you not know how to say no?

Let It Be... Don't Pick Up That Task

This rule is a powerful tactic for avoiding overloading yourself.

Let it be.

I learned this phrase in a meditation course (there *might* be a song by that name, too), but it applies directly to productivity, as well.

You may be thinking, *I can't let it go. I already promised that I would do it.*

That is fine. "Let it be" isn't about dropping tasks. Instead, it is a mindset. It teaches you *not* to pick up unnecessary additional loads. You just don't need to say yes and pick up every item that comes your way.

It's not about letting things go. It's about allowing them *be*. It's not about dropping things; it's about not picking them up in the first place. This is a crucial difference. Like I've said before, a stealthy time-saving ninja *must* travel light. How else could you be productive?

For example, you are reading a news article about a topic and then suddenly you find yourself thirty minutes later in a Wikipedia cave. Did you *really* need to become an expert in a certain celebrity's love life?

Same goes for the latest tech fad. Do you *really* need a third iPad for the living room?

Maybe you've volunteered for something, like helping with intern training at work or baking for your second cousin's bake sale. Why would you take on added responsibility if you haven't handled what you already have on your plate? Sounds like a classic, homemade recipe for failure. Full of sugar and no substance.

Before you take on something, big or small, ask yourself if you really should be taking on that additional obligation or if you should "let it be."

Let It Be... Say No

"Let it be" is an excellent mantra you can use to prevent yourself from taking on unneeded work.

But when it comes to confrontation—person after person asks you to take on additional obligations—*say no.*

Many people don't like to say no. They think it is somehow rude (to value your own time) or that they may hurt the other person's feelings (they can ask someone else). Yet, if you cannot say no, you are essentially saying yes to *everything* that comes your way.

Well, that's definitely not a healthy way to live. Dedication to your most important tasks will make your life far easier and more enjoyable. You have to be able to take care of yourself before taking on tasks from others, young ninja.

Saying no is a skill that requires practice and discipline. It sometimes involves tact and formality, but you can say no.

Ninja Wisdom

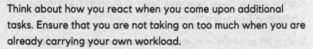

✘ "Let it be" can teach you how to rejoice in what you already have, without overcompensating by taking on others' responsibilities.

✘ Don't drop your tasks, but don't pick up unneeded ones.

✘ Saying no will give you a renewed sense of self-worth.

✘ Do your own work before taking on that of others.

Ninja Training

Think about how you react when you come upon additional tasks. Ensure that you are not taking on too much when you are already carrying your own workload.

✘ Where are you guilty of taking too much on? Why do you take on more than you can handle?

✘ In what situations do you need to "let it be?"

✘ Where do you need to say no more often?

HOW TO TELL IF YOU ARE OVERLOADED

Okay, so you've read the chapter. You now know the benefits of letting things be and saying no, as well as the cons of overfilling your to-do list with responsibilities.

Your next question is natural: "How do I tell if I am overloaded?"

A great way to determine your level of overload is to do an "Obligation Inventory."

Start a list of all the activities, work, chores, and obligations that you are responsible for. Include everything from work to hobbies to family to community requirements. Basically, just brainstorm everything that regularly takes up time on your calendar and in your head.

Only when you have a full list of your obligations can you then determine if you have enough time to do them all. Give each one a time estimate and see if you can realistically fit all your obligations in a typical week. If not, you may need to reduce your load and cut back on some activities.

How many obligations are you carrying? Lightspeed, ninja.

DON'T CREATE YOUR

OWN LIFE FRICTION

If you stop thinking of an issue as a problem,

is it still one?

When was the last time you caused a problem for yourself?

Maybe you forgot to do something. Or blew off an appointment. Or missed a deadline. The truth is that *you* create most of these problems yourself. This can be a bitter pill to swallow. It might even be a large, fishy 650 mg Omega-3 pill. Yes, that bad.

Much of our daily stress and difficulty is the *direct* result of our own actions.

You may be guilty of being your own productivity's worst enemy.

Let's take you to court.

When was the last time your procrastination created an awful situation for you, or a forgotten task had dire consequences?

I call this "life friction." It is the problems, issues, and consequences you create from your actions.

Here are some of the top self-inflicted life frictions:

✦ Forgotten tasks that should have been on your list

✦ Missed deadlines and projects not finished on time

✦ Late to meetings or appointments

✦ Bills not paid on time

✦ Missed opportunities due to procrastination

✦ Repeat errands because you didn't look at your list

- ❧ Rework on a task due to poor planning

- ❧ Not being able to reach someone because you
  lost their number

- ❧ Lost notes because they were misplaced

Creating Life Friction

Life friction is a common symptom of procrastination.

Like the flu, it slows you down. It makes your day-to-day activities far more difficult. If you don't take care of it soon, you may experience symptoms of stress and burnout. No one wants life friction.

The primary carriers of life friction are:

- ❧ **Procrastination:** Putting off tasks often results in more work, but it can also bring consequences such as missed opportunities or financial penalties.

- ❧ **Disorganization:** Not know where things are located or what you need to do results in much-wasted effort and stress.

- ❧ **Lack of priorities:** When you don't put your most important work first, you are going to end up doing trivial tasks that prevent you from delivering satisfying results.

- ❧ **Not making decisions:** Beyond procrastination, not making decisions will hold you back. It can be a form of productivity paralysis (see Tip 17).

These behaviors and their consequences are self-inflicted. You control them and you are responsible for the fallout. *You are the one who creates most of the friction, and thus stress, in your own life.*

The good news is two-fold. First, most of this self-inflicted friction can be addressed simply by using many of the rules in this book. Second, most of the problems you experience are not *nearly* are serious as you make them out to be.

If you are the one causing your problems, then you can also solve them.

Overestimating Problems

What are you stressing about *right* now?

Whether it is your mile-long to-do list, an overdue project, or a forgotten obligation, it's probably *not* the end of the world. It may *seem* like an urgent issue—especially in the moment. However, stress, worry, and panic do *not* solve problems. Ninja skills—focus and action—do.

There are very few true emergencies in life. Except in situations involving serious injury to people's physical safety and well-being, most issues just *aren't* that serious.

Whatever the problem is, ask yourself, "If I stop thinking of this as a problem, is it still one?"

You will be surprised how many problems are just tasks in disguise. Things you need to prioritize and take care of. Even if there is a real penalty for your problem, you *can* deal with the issue and move forward. That is what successful and productive people do. And you are training to become one.

Learn from your perceived problems so that you can avoid them in the future.

Preventing Friction Before It Happens

If you stop and think about your life friction, you are probably guilty of repeating the same situations that cause it. Your productivity and habits are the same, and thus you are getting the same results.

For example, every workplace has that one person who is always late to meetings. It may be a running joke in the office, and the individual probably knows their reputation for being late.

Yet, the situation repeats itself into perpetuity. What will it take for a change? This is what you need to consider in your own life.

What life friction are you guilty of creating? You probably know what it is because it is something that happens regularly. Maybe it's paying bills late or forgetting appointments on your calendar.

To reduce your stress and friction, you need to make a conscious choice and plan to eliminate the self-inflicted behaviors in your lifestyle.

Ninja Wisdom

✖ You create many of the stressors you encounter in life. That means you can also quarantine and eliminate the sources.

✖ Many problems aren't really problems, just tasks that need to be addressed.

✖ There are very few true emergencies in life. Most things you worry about can be ignored.

✖ Getting your work done ahead of time by using proper time management can reduce your life friction.

Ninja Training

Think about how you can reduce your self-created life friction.

✖ Identify three problems that you are creating by your own actions (or lack thereof). Some examples include not paying bills on time, not exercising, and forgetting tasks or appointments.

✖ Identify a remedy for each of your identified life frictions. It could be a reminder or alarm. Maybe even an accountability partner. Just use *whatever* it takes to prevent you from repeating that particular issue—traditional or alternative remedies welcome.

TIP 21

LIVE YOUR LIFE OR YOU

WON'T HAVE ONE

Use your time or lose it.

The sad part is that almost everyone has something that they wish they got around to. Yet, these things seem never to happen.

Time passes. And dreams persist. They are there, nudging us. Not strong enough to act on their own, they cower like ancient immortals. You can't silence your dreams. This is an extremely difficult part of becoming a time management ninja. Your dreams are there, begging for your attention. They want to happen. But you push them into corners, turn off their lights. Unless you feed your dreams, they will continue to cower. Forever. On the sidelines.

Yet, you sit in bed. Blue light masking your face. You swipe ferociously at the screen, past pictures of dreams coming alive for everyone except you.

"The goal is to die with memoires, not dreams."
—Unknown

You Won't Get More Time Later

Are you living your life to the fullest or just letting it slip by?

You say you want more time to spend with your family. Or more time to work out. Or more time to work on your hobbies. Yet, you still spend too much time at work. Too much time doing activities that shouldn't be on your plate in the *first* place.

You tell yourself, "I'll have a life when I get around to it. Or things will settle down eventually."

This is a fallacy. And an immature fantasy.

Life doesn't settle down. It doesn't slow down. And there is *no normal.*

You wish you had more time to spend with your family. Yet, are you spending time with them right now?

You wish you had more time to work out? But, did you exercise yesterday?

You want to write a book? Well, are you writing?

---

*Your life is made up of how you spend your time.
It's that simple.*

Use Your Time or Lose It

You often see this with successful business individuals who neglect themselves and their family. They wish they had more time to spend time with their loved ones. Yet, they are making choices every day to spend their time elsewhere. They don't take care of their families or themselves.

If you squander your time and don't spend it on the things that matter, you will lose those things.

I am always saddened when I hear people who have lost their spouses or family. Inevitably they say things like, "If I had only spent more time with them instead of at work."

Don't wait for a shocking event to happen to truly appreciate what matters to you. Shock yourself every day into doing what you love, and being with who you love.

Remember Your Life is Yours

In these twenty-one tips I have given you the necessary training in decision-making and action-orientation to turn into a time management ninja.

The final tip is a reminder that you have time, but it's up to *you* to actually use it.

Quite frankly, people *just don't spend their time well.* They waste their days on meaningless activities or even destructive ones. Sometimes they let other people steal it for their own use.

Most importantly? *They don't spend it on the things that matter them.*

Turn FOMO to JOMO

In our ultra-connected world, one phrase you hear often is FOMO, or Fear Of Missing Out. It's a silent attacker. You're assaulted by it when you instantly pick up your phone and see not only what all your friends are doing...but what everyone else and their mother is doing.

It's a wasted time and effort to try to live up to other people's lives.

FOMO has always existed, but with our phones and the Internet, it has exploded by several orders of magnitude.

The secret here is to *live your own life.* Do you really care what some celebrity is ranting about? Or what clothes they are selling this week?

Instead, spend your time on the pursuits and endeavors that you deem exciting and essential.

Turn FOMO in to JOMO, or the Joy of Missing Out. Become so involved in your own pursuits and passions that you will happily turn down invitations or social media scrolling in order to do what makes you happy instead.

You Have to Spend Your Time

This isn't meant to be a sad chapter. Instead, it is a positive wake-up call and reminder that you will have to spend your time.

Each day we get the same amount of time.

24 hours. 1440 minutes. 86,400 seconds.

They are yours for the taking. And each day your clock is replenished.

Yet, these minutes and hours are fleeting. (Sometimes they seem to *fly* by...)

Spend it on what is important.

Spend it on those that you love.

Spend it on big goals.

Spend it on *yourself*.

Stop telling yourself that you don't have enough time.

Yes, you *do*. It's how you are spending your time that makes all the difference.

If you don't live your life fruitfully, then you won't have one.

Live for today. Live in the present. And always spend your time wisely.

Ninja Wisdom

✖ Live in the present. Note the past. Plan for the future.

✖ Don't give into FOMO—live *your* life, not that of others.

✖ Make choices and move forward with them all the way.

✖ If you don't spend time wisely and ninja-style, you won't have time.

✖ Don't let people steal your time—it's yours.

Ninja Training

Make sure that you are living your *own* life. Not trying to live up to someone else's or measuring against some non-existent standard. Take a hard look at your time and make sure you are spending it on what matters to you.

✖ Where do you wish you were spending more time in your life? It could be with loved ones or on yourself, your hobbies, goals, etc.

✖ How does FOMO affect your daily life? Do you spend time on things just to keep up with others? What could you ignore or cut out to reduce your FOMO and embrace JOMO?

✖ What can you do to generate time-mindfulness?

✖ What people or activities do you wish to spend more time on?

✖ What do you need to cut out or spend less time on?

✖ What could you do to live a more purposeful life?

✖ What obstacles are preventing you from spending *your* time on *your* life?

MAXIMIZE YOUR LIFE

If you have been neglecting yourself and your personal life, it can be difficult to jump back into it.

Being conscious about your time and how you spend it is the first step. Then, you can start to decide how you want to spend it.

Here are ten tips to help ensure you are living your ninja life to the fullest:

1. **Pay attention:** It is amazing how many people go through their day without paying attention to what they are doing. Be present. Pay attention to what you are doing and whom you are with.

2. **Turn off the electronics:** Don't let your gadgets be an electronic leash for your life. You don't need to be tethered to them 24/7. If you are spending more time with your phone than your loved ones, you have a problem.

3. **Take chances:** If you aren't taking chances, you aren't going to accomplish new levels of achievement. Be bold with your time. You won't always win, but you will surprise yourself more often than not.

4. **Be action-oriented:** You have to be active to be productive. Don't let procrastination and laziness take over your life. Putting things off until tomorrow leads to permanent procrastination.

5. **Be intentional with your time:** Be conscious with your time. Don't waste it merely because you don't know what you should be doing or are disorganized.

6. **Don't let others steal your time:** Time is your most valuable resource. You should protect it with as much vigor as you do with your money. You don't have to let others steal it. Say no, and be firm when others are trying to take your time.

7. **Share your time with those who matter most:** The best way to build relationships with those who matter to you is to spend time with them. Just hanging out. Talking. Doing things together. This is one of the most important ways to live your life to the fullest.

8. **Spend time on yourself:** Don't forget about yourself when it comes to your time. Have a hobby. Spend time on self-improvement or just on writing in your journal. Time to enjoy what you like to do!

9. **Invest some of your time:** You can't save up time, but you can invest it in activities that pay dividends in the future. Exercise, planning, and getting organized are great examples of ways to spend your time. Each of these will make you more productive in the future.

10. **Live your life:** Your life is ultimately the sum of how you spend your time. Live your life each and every day. Life isn't about saving time for later. (That doesn't exactly *work*.) Use your time each and every day to create your own life.

MANAGE YOUR TIME,

MANAGE YOUR LIFE

I hope that these 21 time management tips have provided you with the necessary tips, tactics, and stealthy ways to approach your personal productivity and become a true time management ninja!

They are the result of my twenty-plus years studying how to be efficient and effective while minimizing effort. (That's a lot of time ninja training.) After all, managing your time shouldn't be a chore—it should be a *natural* part of your day. When you value your time, you will be more present in your life and all of its wonderful activities.

As you improve your own habits, you will find that these tips are the bedrock foundation for mastering time management. As you progress you will develop your own strategies and ninja weapons to maximize your time.

Here are a some of my favorite lifehacks that I have developed from these rules:

✤ **You never forget your keys:** If you are concerned about leaving something behind, take your keys out of your pocket or purse and place them with the item. This is particular useful in public places like restaurants and doctor's office. If you put your keys on the countertop with your sunglasses, you won't get very far without them. Haven't left my keys behind in years!

✤ **The early bird writes the email:** The best time of day to *send* emails is very early in the morning. When I send emails at four o'clock, they are *on the top* of people's inboxes when they arrive at work. This greatly increases your chances of a response.

✤ **One thing today:** At the top of my daily "Today List," I have a section for "One Thing Today." It is my most important task that must get done no matter what else transpires in my day. This ensures it stays front and center of my focus.

These are just a few ways I have applied the rules to my life.

What are your best time management tips?

I would love to hear how you stay productive at home and work! Please continue the conversation on my website at TimeManagementNinja.com. You can also reach me on Twitter and Instagram using my handle @TMNinja.

The time management ninja journey is a lifelong one. Your training will take you far!

ACKNOWLEDGMENTS

This book was a long time coming. (There are more than just a few time management jokes there...) None of this book would have been possible without the encouragement of my wife, Amy. She has always been behind my hobby. She supported me years ago when I started my platform, blog, and podcast *Time Management Ninja* and to my current speaking engagements and beyond. I dedicate this book to my kids, Piper and Nate (the "original ninjas" who inspired the name). My family's support means everything to me—they are the top priority of my time!

A special thanks to Hyrum Smith who inspired my passion for time management way back when Franklin day planners ruled the business world. Thanks to everyone at Mango Publishing who supported me in this project—Natasha Vera, for your endless patience and guidance and Yaddyra Peralta for your editing expertise. Finally, thanks to all of the individuals who have read the Time Management Ninja blog over the years. When I started with a single half-page blog post, I never expected that my writings would reach millions of people around the world. Thank you for your readership!

ABOUT THE AUTHOR

Craig Jarrow is the founder of Time Management Ninja, one of the leading productivity websites, and host of the podcast that goes by the same name.

He has authored over one thousand articles on time management since 2008, and has been featured in the media such as CBS MoneyWatch, American Express OPEN, *Lifehacker*, *Ask Men*, The Business Insider, IBM Connection, Inc., and *US News and World Report*.

He has also published two eBooks and offers time management course available on his website.

SOURCES

Mind's Limit Found: 4 Things at Once

www.livescience.com/2493-mind-limit-4.html

70 Percent of Adults Rely on Digital Calendars

ecal.com/70-percent-of-adults-rely-on-digital-calendar/

When Successful People Get Up

www.huffpost.com/entry/this-is-when-successful-people-wake-up_b_596d17a3e4b0376db8b65a1a

Survey: The Average American Has Less than Half an Hour of Free Time per Week

www.theladders.com/career-advice/the-daily-task-americans-are-neglecting-the-most

How Much Time Do We Spend in Meetings? (Hint: It's Scary)

www.themuse.com/advice/how-much-time-do-we-spend-in-meetings-hint-its-scary